Soul Searcher: One Man's Quest to Discover His True Identity

Soul Searcher: One Man's Quest to Discover His True Identity

Sydney Harrison

With Marvin Reid

Dedication

I am dedicating this book to the power of love, and all love has to offer. A love that ignites a flame within that gives the power to heal you.

I dedicate this book to the unsung heroes that dedicate their lives to serving others. As the bible says in Matthew 5:16: "In the same way, let your light shine before others, that they may see your good deeds and glorify your Father in heaven."

I dedicate this book to my birth mother, my family, and my community for never giving up on me, and helping me realize the true essence of life and all it has to offer if you just believe.

Finally, I wish to publicly acknowledge my beloved son, Jerrell. Son, mere words cannot express the pride you have brought to me, nor can they begin to describe the love, trust, and commitment we share as father and son. I am deeply indebted to you for allowing me to be your hero, and for you being mine.

May this work stand as the foundation for our family, and I pray that you will continue to reach for your goals and be the man I know you were born to be. I also want to add that a portion of the proceeds from this book will be given to the charitable organizations that are near and dear to my heart.

Table of Contents

"He lifted me out of the pit of despair, out of the mud and the mire.
He set my feet on solid ground and steadied me as I walked along."
– Psalms 40:2 NLT

Introduction

We've all read many compelling stories of courage and have heard of people who overcame great odds. In each of those stories there is a common theme: a strong will to succeed no matter the cost. It seems there is no specific formula that captures the essence of what brings certain people to this place in their life. They seem to exhibit something special that separates them from others and everybody can feel it.

I've been very fortunate in my life, and I'm telling this story with the hope that it opens hearts and minds to appreciate that we all, in fact, have that something special. All we need to do is look inside ourselves, believe in ourselves, accept our destiny, and finally, fulfill it.

I'm not a wealthy person, but I'm rich in family, friends and power- not the type of power that invites arrogance and makes people fear you, but the type of power that can lend influence to changing the world for the better. I'm not a Nobel Laureate, but I've educated myself well, thanks in part to the hard work, determination and the willingness of those placed in my path to help and guide me.

I do not profess to have all the answers to cure many of the social ills that plague us, but I do have a plan that, if embraced by others, will help change the way we care for one another, especially the youngest among us.

The gift of life truly is precious. If it were not for the mercy of God and the love of my family, these words I write may have been silenced long ago when I was an infant. I am a living, breathing, walking, talking miracle with a story to share. It is a story of perseverance and strength told with help from the perspective of those who know me best. My voice is here. I am here.

While there may be some who look at me and say, *what has he done?*, suggesting that I am no one special. There may be some who say I'm just an ordinary man---they're wrong. I'm an ordinary man with an extraordinary story of survival and perseverance. Sure, I would like to have been the man who scored the winning goal in a World Cup Championship, but I am not that man.

Rather, I fought to stay alive when the doctors gave me less than a ten percent chance to survive my birth. I fought through years of struggling with education and therapy to become a competent professional, a loving father, and eventually, a viable candidate for a county council seat in Prince George's County, one of the richest African-American counties in America, but that's only a small part of the story.

This story is also about the love and strength of an amazing family that took me into their home and raised me after I had been abandoned. That family remains a central part of my life, and I will be forever grateful at how they stood by me through so many trials and tribulations. My mother, father, brothers, and sister are major parts of this story. They are the true unsung heroes who gave me the foundation that allowed me to be the man I am today.

This story is not being written for my benefit---I've been fortunate enough to live it all, the good and the bad. I thank you for walking through this journey with me, and I trust that as you read you'll take away something that will be helpful and inspiring to both you and others you meet.

If my story helps just one person who felt that they were on the outside of opportunity but now feels inspired, I have fulfilled my destiny of being a positive influence, one person at a time. We all have an obligation and responsibility to help others, and one of the greatest, most life changing gifts anyone can receive is love. If you don't leave this story with anything else, I pray that you leave understanding the importance of helping others so that they will do the same.

1

Election Night

It had been a very long day that began before the sun arose high in the September sky. I remember feeling as though my hands were lead weights as I tied my tie and looked at myself in the mirror wondering, "What have I gotten myself into?" It was too late for that. I was committed, and knew that no matter what happened later that night, I had run a good, strong, and honest campaign with a persuasive message.

I ran for a seat on Prince George's County Council for District 9 which covers the towns of: Accokeek, Andrews Air Force Base, Aquasco, Baden, Brandywine, Camp Springs, Cheltenham, Clinton, Croom, Eagle Harbor, Fort Washington, Piscataway, and Upper Marlboro.

District 9 comprises over forty percent of the landmass of the county, making Prince George's County one of the most populous counties in the state. Economically speaking, at one time there were more registered owners of BMW automobiles than anywhere else in the world. That should give you a snapshot of the economic status of the area even though there is still a great deal of poverty and despair that has little to do with a bad economy.

Despite the economic status of the area, there are also an abundance of poor and working poor in Prince George's County. We needed more opportunities that will establish higher paying jobs and a better lifestyle for these hardworking families. Even though we live in the richest African American community in the

United States, there are still a lot of people suffering to make ends meet. In addition, we have one of the worst rated school systems in the state of Maryland and a high dropout rate.

During the campaign, I understood that this message spoke to all county residents, not just the privileged. I wanted to be inclusive and speak to what I believed was the heart of Prince George's County: the family.

Political campaigns can be particularly long, grueling and unpredictable. For example, there were always unexpected and unplanned trips to speak with constituents who either wanted to meet me or lend their support to the campaign. My schedule was erratic at best but always stayed focused and purposeful.

I was tired but hopeful on Election Day. Election Day is the final day of campaigning and the most difficult, primarily because, you know that when you awaken the next day either you'll be a county councilman or giving your boss a call to inform him or her that you're returning to work, that is, if you still have a job. If not, you'll be looking for work with everyone else. Losing the race was a prospect I had certainly planned for but wasn't particularly excited about having to experience.

Standing in my campaign headquarters on Main Street in Upper Marlboro, I knew I was facing an arduous night but I had long committed myself and was just waiting for the end, or the beginning to come. I can recall not being scared or even worried. I believed more than anything that the campaign message was a powerful one and that it would resonate with the people of the county and they would support it.

I believed that the thousands of hours spent on my campaign, pressing the flesh and seeking out campaign contributors, would prove successful. My family was very strong during this time as they had been throughout my life and they knew I needed their support now more than ever.

Though I was cool on the exterior, my insides were churning as I watched numbers start rolling in at the bottom of the television screen. By this time, the polls had only been closed five minutes and you would've thought people would still be at polling places finalizing their votes or leaving. Instead, it was quiet and there was not very much chatter among those who had gathered with me to witness this event.

The silence was deafening when I suddenly realized it wasn't quiet at all. There was chatter and movement all around. It just felt quiet to me. What was going on? Was I experiencing some epiphany? Had I fallen into a depression I wasn't aware of? Had the intensity of the moment caused me to block everything out? I don't know what it was but I just know I wasn't myself.

Think about it, day after day, month after month, standing on the sides of main traffic arteries waving at people as cars passed, and going to events where at times, I had to suddenly answer questions I wasn't quite expecting. This is not to mention the countless churches and other places of worship where I attended and spoke, even after I had become extremely exhausted. It was all coming to an end or rather, a crashing halt.

Sure, you could say I was tired, fatigued even, but I knew my race was really just beginning.

I sincerely believe that when people run for office it's not something that happens in a vacuum. Many candidates run for office because of the sincere belief in an ideal. Some lose their way once elected or begin to feel a sort of 'God' complex once in office, but the hope is that most politicians do it to serve the public and continue once in office. I ran because I had seen the very best and worst in the county and I believe in the people of my community. I understand that education is essential to the evolution of humanity, and truly believed that it is indeed the great equalizer. However, it will never truly be equal, as famed educator Horace Mann once said.

Let me explain. We can talk all day about local, state and federal initiatives in education, and ensuring that all children be successful and on and on, but is that what the school systems and politicians really want? If so, I have a series of questions that need to be answered.

First, if there's never been equality in anything on planet Earth, how can there be educational equality? It's a fact that we all learn at different rates and in different ways. We ask teachers to work miracles and graduate every child. We know that if, in fact, they did, there wouldn't be enough jobs to accommodate them.

I'm certainly not suggesting that having every child graduate is not a great goal to shoot for. Of course, more formally educated people is a good thing, but are we being realistic when we suggest that by some magical year all children will be at or about the same level and will have the same level of success? It's a delusion wrapped in a fallacy, surrounded by mass confusion.

I wonder how things will be justified when the vast majority of the country is not even close to achieving that goal. In my view, there has never been true equality in the history of man, primarily because that's the beauty of what makes us human. We're all different. We learn at different rates, some of us are more ambitious than others, and frankly, our world is not set up to handle everything and everyone being the same.

We all have something that makes us uniquely different and special. Accordingly, as adults, teachers, mentors and community leaders, we must make it a point to bring out what makes a child perform at their best. The answer is not just pushing them toward a traditional college which may not capitalize on their strengths.

I will give you an example, because of my learning disabilities I barely made it out of high school. I also felt that college would be too much. I was in a world of confusion so I got a job as a plumber. I always had a mind for fixing things growing up, so I thought this might be a decent choice. Plumbing was something I knew I could do and I was right. I excelled as a plumber's apprentice and it created an opportunity to do something I enjoyed; troubleshooting and fixing things. In my 12 years as a plumber, I learned a lot and I accomplished a lot, including remodeling a bathroom that was featured on HGTV.

The point is, college is not for everyone, but there are other forms of higher education, such as vocational on the job training, which can be just as beneficial for some people. It is also important to focus on preparing our youth for the real world when they are in high school. Then, they would know that even if they did not do well in high school, other opportunities are available to them such as, apprenticeships, internships, trade schools, cosmetology, nursing, and entrepreneurship. The beauty of owning your business is that you can control your destiny. Small businesses, in many ways, are the economic engine to today's economy. Our young people should know that.

Don't get me wrong, I strongly believe that going to college is a great thing and if you have the opportunity and aptitude to attend, you should. Our youth must understand that to reach and achieve your dreams, you will need some form of higher training in something, even if it's not college.

I ran on a platform of access. Students should have access to the best public education we can provide. Parents should not have to stress over their child's education…I'm campaigning again…sorry about that. It truly is a strong belief for me, so I carry it with me everywhere.

There I was on September 14, 2010 standing alone as my supporters were gathered at the Old Town Inn in Upper Marlboro. It was as if I could hear them cheer as my name was called by the political commentators. What was most poignant about this run is that I don't even remember seeing or hearing anything or anyone. I knew people were around but, as I said, I was in an odd place emotionally.

Political election nights are far different from a football game, a basketball game or even a tennis match. In sports, like political contests, there is a winner and a loser, but unlike sports, the winner of a political election will directly impact the lives of his or her neighbors.

Time was starting to tick faster and my hands began to perspire. It seemed as if I couldn't wipe them off enough. I tried going outside to get some air but that did not help. I just wanted it to be over so that I could get to work for the people, and it wouldn't be long before I would have my wish. My intent was to win. I didn't think about losing. All I could think about were the plethora of things that I was dedicated to accomplishing for the people once I was elected. The voices of the people were what I was planning to take with me all the way to the Prince George's County Council to make sure their concerns were heard.

As 85% of the precincts had reported in, I was well within striking range of winning my first election. There were ten candidates, and with a seemingly large pool of that kind, the vote would likely be spread thin, so every single vote counted.

Someone walked over and handed me a soda. My body was so numb that I don't even remember the flavor. I held onto the can, and found myself squeezing it as hard as I could without it buckling and spilling all over me.   The time had come for the results to be as close to final as they would be that night. I looked at the tally and saw I was a little more than a thousand votes short and breathed a sigh of relief. I think it was physical and emotional exhaustion more than anything but at least, I knew the results. I collected myself, nodded my head and watched as the projected winners were named. I was not among them. I lost.

Those who were there to support me had worked extremely hard to keep me emotionally strong and mentally balanced. It was no easy task. Unlike the marathon runner who gets less than a mile away from the finish line and has to stop because of cramps, I went all the way to the wire without stopping. But I still came up a little short, and was devastated.

Soccer, one of my true loves, prepared me well. In soccer, you're literally running for ninety minutes, only stopping moments at a time for shots on goal and/or penalties. There is no time out to speak of and you'd better keep moving or you may get scored on, knocked down, or both. I had experienced loss before but this campaign loss felt different. In so many ways, it was uncharted waters for me.

Part of me wants to say I stood off to the side for a moment, collected my thoughts and celebrated the process with my supporters, friends, and family. The truth is that I went off alone to cry. I cried because I was tired from the journey, but also because I arrived at an important destination. It wasn't the destination I planned for, but someone said to me once that "God always laughs at our plans." I had no idea of the significance that statement would have in my life until that day.

Losing a political election is tantamount to the death of a close friend. They say it remains in your heart even after it's over. Political campaigns can be grueling and very strenuous, but once it's in your system, it's there. When the campaign was over, I began to miss it; even the bad parts. I missed being part of a process that gave me the opportunity at that time to really make a difference. I also missed sharing my platform and solutions with the people.

My love for people and this county made it a very heartbreaking loss. I went through many of the stages of grief, and that grieving process was a lot like experiencing the loss or death of a close friend. I loved the whole process and its evolution, even though the outcome was not what I would have liked it to be.

I had to now figure out what I was going to do with the next few years, and how I could further the causes that were important to me until the next election cycle. Though I may have lost the first one, I was on the cusp of taking a county council seat from someone who had been campaigning for years before I began. I eliminated their lead in just nine months, and garnered just above twenty-percent of the vote. Even that proverbial silver lining of doing so well on the first run wasn't enough to console me at that moment.

Winning is nice, but losing wasn't all bad. It gave me an appreciation and understanding of what our President, members of Congress and our state leaders have to go through, just on a slightly smaller scale.

Facing the uncertainty of "normal" life, my thoughts immediately turned to my teenage son; a bright, energetic and impressionable young man. He had grown so much, both mentally and physically, in a year. I was now left with the prospect of sharing the bad news with him. My son and I have an unspoken bond. Unlike many fathers who may give reams of advice with nothing more, my son and I share a much deeper connection. It's like we know what the other is thinking and feeling without having to say it.

When I finally did see him, the hug I received told me, "Dad, it's OK, we'll get 'em next time." That was all I needed. When he hugged me, I melted inside. I wanted him to see his dad victorious and proud of having won. It was not to be but in that moment, I could not have been prouder to see how much my son had matured in the span of one year.

The compassion and empathy he showed really made me see how much we are alike and how much he had grown. I saw that failing and losing was one of the most important lessons I could teach him. In life, you will have major disappointments, setbacks and heartbreaks, but life is about how you get up, after being knocked down. It's about how you respond, comeback, and show that you cannot be broken. Win or lose, we all have the desire to be a champion to someone.

I knew I had to get myself together because there were dozens of people I needed to thank, so I went into the bathroom and threw some cold water on my face. In a way, it was an opportunity to get a good look at myself. It was interesting-I didn't see a loser, which made me ask the question, "What does a 'loser' look like?" I wasn't quite sure what the answer was and at that moment I didn't care very much. I knew I had won a personal victory which meant more to me than actually winning the seat.

My campaign headquarters was quiet and somber, except the sound of the television touting the winners of the contest and the commentators discussing the turnout. For some reason, far fewer people tend to come out for local elections. Perhaps they incorrectly believe that their vote doesn't matter or that local elections aren't as important as national ones.

Think what you will about politics, but in my opinion our form of government, our system, and our way of life is about people helping people. There were still people out there who needed help. I needed to find a way to help them and I would, but I knew that I would have a smaller platform and would have to do it in smaller numbers.

I can think of no greater position to be in than that of serving others. It was instilled in me from as far back as I can remember that the things we do for others directly impact what happens in our own lives.

Thankfully, I have been blessed with a wonderful family and great friends who have sustained me through every part of my life. I feel as though my life is really just beginning and by the time I really hit my stride, I can only imagine what's in store. I remind myself everyday that this life I have is a gift and I made a promise that I would use it for the betterment of mankind and not for my own vainglory.

Political life can often be a stumbling block to personal growth. We've seen many times, especially in recent years, where our elected officials and even members of the clergy forget that they are servants of the public and their values become compromised.

As I stared into their eyes, I saw their deep emotion from the loss and felt a sincere gratitude to all who had sacrificed their time for me and were in the trenches with me as we fought for a message that resonated with the people. We fought so that our voices would be heard, and so that our faces and names would be a part of the process. It choked me up, made the hairs on my arms stand up, and made me think how my story and life granted me this opportunity, which was very special to me.

As I share my life and story with you, my wish is that you will see that hope is always alive and all that you need is a spark to shine your light into the world. As I take you on this journey and retrace the foot prints in the sand of life, you will see where the floods of the storms and the elements of life tried to turn love into rust.

2

Left Alone

On September 17, 1974, I was born to a drug-addicted mother who had been raped at gunpoint. No, that's not the beginning of a Hollywood movie. That's the way I came to be.

My birthmother was just a teenager. Like many teens, she was rebellious and lived life the way she wanted. At the time, she had no clue as to the negative results that would come from this way of life. After being raped and becoming pregnant with me, she continued to drink alcohol, use drugs, and smoke cigarettes. My birthmother did not have prenatal care, and she continued to engage in destructive behavior until I was born. Then, she abandoned me at the hospital.

I weighed only two pounds, and the doctors gave me a less than ten percent chance of survival. Aside from being well under the average baby weight, I had gangrene in my intestines, a herniated bowel, and a host of other physical issues. If you've ever seen tiny premature babies in the hospital, then you have a pretty good idea of what I looked like. My situation was even more dire because I was also extremely sick and had my first surgery days into my new life.

So how did this happen? Your guess is as good as mine. Our birth is one of the great mysteries of life. None of us truly know why we arrive on this earth with the circumstances and parents we are given. Physiologically, it's very simple. There's sperm and an egg that combine to create a person. As we learn and grow, the best and worst of our mother and father are often within us. It is up to us to make the very best life we can with the cards we've been dealt.

In my case, life started particularly difficult because of my physical condition. I managed to survive my birth and the poor health that ensued, but there were still issues of custody. I was a sick infant. I was alone in a hospital with no one to take me home or to care for me.

Now that you know how I came into this world, imagine for a moment being in a dark room. You cannot see, and there is sound all around you. Then, imagine that the voices you hear are indistinguishable and, sound like a foreign language. You're aware of your surroundings, but you're unable to speak so you just lie there. Then, out of nowhere, comes a clearly distinguishable voice asking, "If I give you life, what are you going to do with it?"

Call me crazy, but I still hear that voice today. Without getting too deeply entrenched in religion and spirituality, it was a voice that could only be described as majestic and powerful. The command of that voice told me that it was someone or something with the power to improve my situation, or end it. Because I was a very tiny infant with no defenses or speaking ability, I was in no condition to answer. As time went on, I would hear that voice more clearly, especially as I began to realize that I was in fact alive.

To understand who I am, you have to understand how I got here. When you consider how I was conceived, where I came from biologically, you will understand why I am thankful beyond measure to be able to learn the importance and appreciation of family.

The year 1974, the year I was born, was a difficult year in America. The country was mired in the Vietnam Conflict; facing the first U.S. President to ever resign; and saddled with an economy that mirrored the Great Depression. I wonder how people survived it. My birthmother is an interesting woman. In my talks with her I learned so much about her life and what happened to her. She was born in 1957, in the heart of Pennsylvania Dutch Country, to an eighteen- year-old woman. Ever since her birth, she felt different and apart from her siblings. The eldest of three children, she grew up in the Golden Age of America with Ed Sullivan, Elvis Presley and hot rods.

There was a lot of dysfunction in her family. Alcoholism and chaos were norms that she constantly had to endure. My grandmother got married in a so-called "shotgun wedding", which was normal at the time, but there were always questions about my mother's paternity. Apparently, my grandmother was an exceptionally beautiful woman. According to my birthmother, my grandmother's beauty would get her into trouble. There were always whispers and speculation that she was not her father's daughter, but another man's. As you can already see, the negative pathology of the family had been an issue for some time.

My grandmother had three children at a very young age, but still wanted to live her life. This did not make things easy. During the first five years of my birthmother's life, she said that she felt "different." She loved her parents, but her father was in the Air Force and gone all the time. There were different babysitters constantly, and it wasn't a happy home. My birthmother recalls, "My dad came back from France and I remember watching him chase my mother around the house with a butcher knife." It might be hard to believe for some, but even back then, 911 existed. She told me that she called 911 for help.

My birthmother ran away from home for the first time when she was five years old. She said she went to a neighbor's house. It sounds like a silly runaway plan, but it was all she could think of at such a young age. She did whatever she could to escape the realities of her home life. She missed her dad and wasn't exactly sure what she needed or wanted out of life. Even as a young child, though, she knew her home was not where she wanted to be. It just wasn't a happy and safe place.

By the time she was ten years old, my birthmother began acting out even more. Her home life did not improve, and she became increasingly more agitated. She would do things for negative attention, and running away was her coping mechanism of choice. In school, she was teased by other children. It was so bad that, in an effort to have the other children like her, she would steal money from her parents to buy them candy.

Though she never got into trouble with the law, she was a handful for her parents. When her parents split, it just perpetuated the environment of mistrust and dysfunction she had experienced throughout her young life.

One of the most significant parts of her childhood is seeing her mom with other men while still married to her father. It still affects her today. The nurturing we all need, crave and seek out as children was not there for her at all. Her future was shaping as quickly as her past and present would allow, and it was only a matter of time before it would become disastrous.

As a pre-teen, my birthmother felt like she was a mistake and was always saddled with adult responsibilities. Her mom worked at a beauty shop during the day and was a cocktail waitress in the evenings, making my birthmother directly responsible for the care of her siblings. This is far too much to put on a child, don't you think? It's been more than forty years, and we hear the same type of story play out time and again.

She was a young child with problems that went ignored. She was too young to speak for herself, and no one was brave enough to intervene and help. She was abused and saddled with far too much responsibility. Even today, we as a community hear about children in abusive situations or trying to raise themselves because their parents are absent, working or otherwise unavailable.

In the early 1970s, my birthmother moved with her siblings and mom into a trailer that she described as "God-awful." Her behavior had gotten worse, and no amount of discipline stemmed the tide of her decline. "Incorrigible" is a fitting word to sum it up.

One night, when my mother was almost thirteen, her mother's then boyfriend came in from a baseball game and saw her seated on the couch. He proceeded to make mature advancements towards her and attempted to, "mess around" with her. She told her mom, and her response was that he was drunk and thought my birthmother was his girlfriend. She doesn't think that was the case because he had driven from Philadelphia, PA to Hershey, PA, which is a good two-hour drive. She felt violated and knew that her mother didn't need or want her. She felt that she could never do anything right, or anything that would make her mother want her.

It was an incredibly painful and difficult time for my birth mother because she was enduring difficulties that many adults don't have to face in a lifetime--and she was barely thirteen years old.

After being sent to a group home, my birthmother felt unwanted, rejected and full of despair. She hadn't committed a crime or hurt anyone. She just wanted to be loved, nurtured and cared for like any other child.

To put this story in its proper perspective, you need to know that these are not my words, but those of my birth mother. I am not paraphrasing or even sensationalizing her story. I am merely outlining her life so that you can understand the circumstances I was born into. This may be difficult to read, but I am sure you can imagine that it felt even worse to hear it.

Behind every young person who finds themselves in trouble at school or at odds with the law, there is a story. While their story may be more or less dramatic than mine, inside that person beats a heart that was born pure, good, and blameless. I ask that you please set aside any condemnation or preconceived notions you may have. How many of us would actually have been able to survive and endure the difficulties my birthmother faced? How many of us would be able to endure the tragedies that have occurred in the lives of many other nameless, faceless people?

My birth mother would routinely act out in order to find someone who would give her the attention she desperately needed and wanted. Again, and true to form, she bolted from the group home by opening up a window and sliding down a rain spout.

She said that she ran away because she "had been beaten up by a boy there." Though the boys and girls were segregated, she managed to get into somewhat of a scrape. The conditions at the group home were deplorable and although she had not committed a crime, she was placed in a juvenile detention center for about three months. In those days, it wasn't uncommon for a child to be shuttled from place-to-place and left to fend for themselves. She was a child full of misery that needed a break and some help, but there was none to be found.

She was fortunate to appear before a sympathetic judge who saw that she had not committed any crime. He wanted to offer her an opportunity to be placed somewhere other than the typical bad-girl's home. She ended up in a foster home in Paradise, PA, Dutch Country.

While living there, she was further damaged emotionally by a conversation she overheard between her foster parent and another person. The gist of the conversation was that my birthmother was yet another mouth to feed in a house that was already crammed with seven children, and neither the state nor her family offered anything in the way of financial support. My birthmother felt like she was an unwanted burden.

As you can probably guess, it was only a matter of time before she had enough and ran away yet again. She ran because she always felt like such a burden and always wondered why no one wanted her, loved her, or even tried to be kind to her. As a teenager, she was fraught with grief and despair. She was a teenage child alone in the world. She learned to care less about life and herself than even those around her. Little did she know her life would take a turn that would make all of her prior experiences seem like a walk in the park.

My birthmother moved around a lot through the year after leaving the group home, and in the course of so much moving, she met a guy from the past. He was in the Army, stationed at Ft. Bragg, in Fayetteville, NC. He had been writing her for some time and kept up with her in spite of the fact that she moved so much.

When she ran away from the foster home, she pretty much made up her mind that she wasn't going back. She decided to make her way to North Carolina to visit the guy, but with no intentions of being with him intimately or having a romantic relationship with him.

When she arrived in Fayetteville, the guy saw that she was still underage and decided he wanted nothing to do with her. She ended up sleeping in bus stations, gas stations or wherever she could. She hitch-hiked a lot and would always hope there would be someone around to put her up for the night.

Ultimately, she had no one but herself. She realized that hitch-hiking and taking shelter with people she barely knew was dangerous, but she had no choice. She told me that she hitch-hiked from as far as North Carolina to Maine and back, without incident. This, however, would change, and her hitch-hiking experience would soon take a turn for the worst.

While she doesn't remember the exact date, my birthmother got a fake ID and started stripping, which she usually did while high on acid, the popular drug of the day. She entered a "Go-Go Dancer" contest and danced because she was often hungry and had no money. She made use of the only thing of value she thought she had - her body. She did what she had to do to survive.

My birthmother said she also had to eat out of garbage cans because things had gotten so bad. She thought she would starve to death, and had never felt a more desperate feeling up to that point in her life. While she isn't at all proud of the way she lived her young life, she is proud that she survived. She firmly believes it strengthened her to be the woman she is today.

Due to the passage of time and the regular use and abuse of drugs, my birthmother's details of my conception are sketchy, but she talks about that one particular day in February that was terribly cold. Before I go into this part of the story, I must stop to warn you that, even though it is very important for my birthmother's full story to be told in order for you to understand who I am, this portion of the story, in particular, may be very difficult for some to read. My birthmother was leaving a part of town generally known as a red light district, a place where prostitutes and drug dealers would encamp. It was toward the end of the Vietnam Conflict, and there were U.S. servicemen everywhere. She was still hitch hiking and got into a car with two men. She had no fear. After all, she had done this many times before. My birthmother was a young teenager lost in the dangerous elements of the world that consumed her young life, and didn't thoroughly understand that the decision she had just made would scar her for the next several decades.

As she was in the process of giving them directions, she quickly realized that something was amiss. She remembers getting a cold and creepy feeling from the men in the car. She spoke very gingerly as she was giving them directions, but she soon noticed that the directions were being ignored. These two men had another agenda.

She became very scared and the thought that something bad would happen suddenly became very real. She tried to stay calm but noticed that her body began to shake uncontrollably with nervousness. Before she could react, the barrel of a gun went into her mouth and fear had become her newest traveling companion. It was a difficult moment to recall, and she remembers it with considerable trepidation.

They drove for several miles down Interstate 95 outside of Fayetteville to an old abandoned airfield, and it seemed as though they knew where they were going. It also appeared to her that it wasn't the first time they had done whatever they were about to do. The man driving began to curse and scream. He then stopped the car and got out.

She remembers that one of the men wasn't particularly attractive. He was a Caucasian man with rotten teeth. There were Georgia tags on the car, and the men appeared to be between twenty-five and thirty years old. It was dark and difficult to make out the description of the other man in the car, but he was definitely African American and shorter than the man she could clearly see. Either way she knew she was out-matched.

My birthmother believed she was about to die and that her life, as bad as it had been, was about to be over. It was an indescribable feeling for her. In her mind, all she could think at the time was, out of all the people in the world, why is this happening to me? No one cared about her, and she felt that regardless of what was coming, it didn't matter—no one would miss her anyway. With fear gripping and siphoning her strength, she began to repeatedly beg for her life, to no avail.

They opened up the back door of the car and dragged her out by her ankles.

As she was fighting to be released, one of the men began to beat her and smack her over the head with the butt of his gun. She thought about running, but she was knocked down and both men now towered over her. She remembers yelling, "Please, please, stop." She was dazed and confused by the sheer terror of what was about to happen. She remembers thinking, is this what my poor little life has come to in my short period on this earth?

The first man, the Caucasian man, began to unzip his pants, while the other man shoved the cold barrel of the gun so far down her throat that she began to choke. The Caucasian man began to forcefully thrust himself into her young body, as tears were streaming down her face. She remembers trying to scream, but there was no one around to hear. It was also clear that she was in an area no one would stumble upon anytime soon. The African American man then began to inflict the same pain on her. They took repeated turns raping her, over and over.

After the two men were done, they were trying to figure out what to do. One of the men said, "Let's kill her." My birthmother began to plead for her life, "Please, please, please. I won't tell anyone. Please let me live." Finally, the other man said, "Come on we have to get out of here. Let's go." They both fled.

They left her lying on the ground with the soil of hatred all over her. She remembers feeling unwanted, beat up, and ravaged by these heinous acts of violence. Violated, cold, shivering, clothes torn, and with nowhere to go, she just began to walk as the sun set on a cold February day in North Carolina.

My birthmother was candid about her sex life and mentioned that, while she was in fact sexually active, she hadn't been with anyone else at the time of the rape. That cold February day is when I was conceived.

She never saw the men again but, needless to say, they changed her life forever. She still wonders about the women that may have been led back to that place and never left.

My birthmother had been severely beaten, gang-raped, and left alone in a field miles away from help--and she never told anyone. No one believed anything she said before and she didn't think that they would start now. She took a bus back to her foster home in Pennsylvania, but of course, was still consumed with what just happened. My birthmother vowed never to go back to her foster home, but after being raped, she just wanted to be somewhere familiar and "normal" for her.

As I considered the severity of her situation, I thought about my own. I'm a grown man now, a father, and a responsible member of society, yet I am the product of a rapist. Bad things happen to people all the time but I had been conceived during the commission of a violent felony. This is not at all to compare my experience to my birthmother's. It is only to provide further insight into my life, which must have been affected by how I was conceived and cared for prior to my birth.

Even now, I sit and think of the events my birthmother described and can hardly believe it. It is as if it happened to someone else. I feel a deep sense of sadness for my birthmother and the horror she experienced, however, now, more than ever, I fully understand my responsibility to bring light to this dark situation. My hope is that through her pain, I can be a blessing to someone else.

My birthmother learned that she was pregnant shortly after returning to yet another foster home. She quickly realized she could not stay, so she again left the foster home and returned to North Carolina, the only other place she was familiar with. Very shortly after getting off the bus, she met a man in the bus station who was trolling for drugs. As she explained, she was easy prey because she was visibly fearful and vulnerable.

Not knowing what to do next, my birthmother decided to resume dancing. She spent the night in a motel with the man she met at the bus station. With him, she got drunk off of gin. Unfortunately, she was yet again being abused by another man. Even more unfortunate is that she found it to be a relatively safe and familiar place.

The man had served a year in Vietnam in lieu of a stretch in the penitentiary. This was the result of an interesting plea bargain which was prevalent at the time. The plea bargain made it possible for people who were accused of a crime to have the option of going to war instead of jail, according to my birth mother.

Their relationship was as disastrous as any other she had been in. He was a heroin addict who turned her out into the streets to be a prostitute. Her attitude had become one of apathy and hopelessness because of everything she experienced at such a tender age.

What's most significant to me throughout my conversation with her is that while she smoked marijuana and drank alcohol throughout her pregnancy, she honestly tried not to use hardcore drugs, even though she wasn't always successful.

With no prenatal care to speak of, my birthmother seriously considered having an abortion. She wanted no parts of a child who had been forced into her through a violent rape, especially not knowing which rapist was the father. Her man, and pimp, gave her money for an abortion, and she went to the clinic for the procedure.

She remembers that it was a nice day, and she was at the tail end of her first trimester. There were protesters outside of the clinic screaming, calling her a murderer, and waving signs. When she walked in, she felt like she was in a butcher shop. Women were crying, and she immediately began to doubt what she was about to do. She felt a sense of coldness as she waited for the doctor to see her and perform the abortion.

She told me how frightened she was. She was all alone and just did not want to bring a baby into the world that way--through a violent rape. She began to wrestle with her feelings of loneliness and sadness. With that being the case, how could she love a baby?

As time passed, she began to feel sharp pains in her womb, causing her to curl up into the fetal position. Was this my first fight for life? My birthmother noticed the time as it passed. It had already been forty-five minutes and the doctor still had not come to the waiting room for her.

Finally, a doctor came and my birthmother was shown a video about the procedure she was about to have. The video was supposed to prepare her for the abortion. Instead, it was intensely cold and all she could think about was having me out of her.

The coldness of the documentary and the long wait were starting to set in mentally. The table she was placed on was so cold, and everything seemed to be about procedure, not comfort. The coldness of the table worked up from the bottom of her feet through her entire body and began to give her goose bumps. The hairs on her arms began to stand up. She was all alone and forced to make a life or death decision as a teen.

After seeing the women walking out, many of them crying, and hearing my heartbeat, a light bulb went off. She said to herself, This baby has a heart, feet, and can probably feel, so what am I doing? She began to cry, and as the doctor walked in, my birthmother said, "I just can't do it." She jumped off the table, quickly dressed and walked out of there. She had saved my life.

My birthmother went on to express that she had been through a lot of things in her young life and it became unmanageable. Things became even more complicated because she returned to the man she was staying with. She explained to him that she couldn't go through with the abortion and he responded by severely beating her. He would punch her in places that were not visible, sometimes knocking her out. There were times she remembers him putting lit cigarettes out on her skin. He treated her more like property, not a person. He kept her around primarily because her prostituting provided him with his drug money.

My birthmother talked candidly about how the man she was with knocked her out on several occasions. There was nothing that was going to stand in the way of his next fix. He had complete control of her life. She got used to him being high, and she always knew when he was. When he was high, he was in a completely different state of mind and became a different person.

Her coping mechanism was to drink, smoke weed, and get high on acid--all while pregnant with me. Hallucinogenic drugs gave her a way to escape the situation in her mind, but the reality was that she couldn't physically escape. She was completely dependent on this man and needed drugs just to cope.

As her life continued to spiral out of control, my birthmother left North Carolina with the man. There was a warrant for his arrest in North Carolina, so they went north to Washington, DC. She was about six months pregnant with me and extremely worried. Although she didn't want me, she believed I would be OK anyway.

My birthmother talked about the night before I was born. She was beaten by the man she was with, but she doesn't exactly remember what he had beaten her for that time. She was taking a bath when he came into the bathroom. He took her head and held it under the water until she nearly passed out. Then, he dragged her out of the tub and slammed her head onto the floor. He was bold and brazen, telling her that he killed many people in Vietnam and had no problem killing her.

Following the beating, she passed out and thanks to the efforts of a Good Samaritan; she was rushed to Greater Southeast Hospital. She was told that her uterus was contracted and the baby would be coming soon. The faces of the nurses around her let her know how the grave the situation was. The baby might not survive the birth. Fortunately, I did survive, and my birthmother was relieved. This relief was fleeting because she was immediately told that I needed a blood transfusion.

She did not know what to do, so she phoned her parents collect. They refused the charges. The man she was with was present the day I was born at Greater Southeast.

The nurses and doctors wanted to talk to her, but the man sensed trouble and got her out of the hospital.

She left me there alone; not knowing what was to become of me for years to come.

3

Family Values
(Who Am I?)

As you can see I faced a multitude of different health issues that I had to overcome during the first moments of my life. But even with all of the challenges I faced, still a plan was put in place where God had me protected by the covering of his arms. I would learn the true meaning of family regardless of how I came into the world. That process and lesson would repeat itself for many years to come throughout my life and it still does today. Who will be my protector, who will nurse me back to health, and who will love me in a way that is unconditional that would have the makings to heal this little fighter and give me a chance at life?

I was born with a host of health issues and children born with these types of ailments rarely survive, even with modern medicine. This is primarily because they have to fight so hard on their own, physically and mentally, when they have not a clue of what that means or how to do it. How did I do it? I can only say that it through the grace of God. I am sure of it. I've heard people throw the word miracle around when hearing my story but I can assure you that I am no miracle. The way I see it, I'm exactly what I was meant to be because God wouldn't have it any other way.

I brought God into the equation, and I will do so throughout my story because only God could take a life that began like mine and make it whole.

My first surgery came when I was days old. I was opened up, and the diseased portion of my intestine was removed. At the time,

I was in the care of the medical staff at Children's Hospital in Washington, DC. I was transported there by Greater Southeast Hospital. I was in for the fight of my life, literally, and I fought for every breath. For the first three months of my life, I didn't have a mother or a father. I was placed in foster care with my pre-adoptive parents, the Harrisons. They went through all of the steps to become suitable foster parents in a process that took place long before I was born. I was only supposed to be with them for approximately six weeks, but six weeks turned into two-and-a-half years. At some point after that, social services tried to remove me from their home. This is where things became extremely complicated. As if the circumstances under which I became a foster child weren't enough, there were social issues at play that weren't making my situation any better. The Harrisons are Caucasian, and I am bi-racial. In those days, I was considered a person of color and was required to be placed in an African American household.

Even as a young child, I can still remember feeling the warmth of my adoptive mother. From this point forward, I will simply refer to her as my Mom. I remember when she would hold me close, I would hear her heartbeat and know I was safe.

I was brought into a family that had been long established. The family consisted of three children: my brother John, 7, my sister Heather, 4; and my brother Josh, who was 2. As a two-year-old child, I was calling my parents Mommy and Daddy and was treated like a brother by my siblings. Things were going so well that the Harrisons made the decision to adopt me and make me a part of their family for good. They fought for me for over two years, and I was adopted at about four-and-a-half years old. They named me Sydney Jerome Harrison.

My mother would never really talk about the process my family went through to adopt me or what happened in the courtroom. It broke her heart, but my mother, standing five foot even, had taken on the system and never backed down. At that time, my adoption was a very racially sensitive issue, and the court could only see things one way. My parents, however, knew the difference between right and wrong.

The bottom line is that the court system wanted to take me from the loving family I had known and place me with a family of color, out of fear that I would lose my identity. Should color supersede love? All my mother knew was that she had grown to love me as her child and wanted to make sure that I had the chance to have a good life. She wanted me to be a part of a loving family.

Imagine how emotionally draining it would be to know how deeply you loved your child and then to hear things like "this child could potentially lose his identity" or "we need to find him a new family"? At the end of the day, all that really matters is that they loved me and wanted me in their family.

In 1978, my siblings attended school in Prince George's County, and I was formally introduced to education. My grandmother, who I called Nana, was a librarian at the primary school I had just entered, Henson Valley Montessori School. My family quickly realized I had some learning disabilities, but in those days, there was little understanding about special education and how to educate children with challenges like mine. I was sent to Harmony Hall Elementary School, and my Nana continued to work with me to make sure I did not fall behind. She was the first one to introduce me to sports and a soccer ball. Soccer became my first love. Harmony Hall, located in Fort Washington, Maryland, had a special education wing for all special-needs students, but it was separate from the general student population. There were two teachers and an aide in each classroom.

The teachers gave us a great deal of one-on-one attention, and we learned everything slowly and deliberately. Looking back, I believe one of the reasons I have managed so well in life is that they taught me how to work smart and work hard. I was taught to complete one task before beginning another and how to focus, which were struggles for me growing up.

If you've ever spent time with a child who has a learning disability, you know the frustrations they face, especially when they want so desperately to do things the right way, the first time. I can remember writing my letters backwards and continuing to do so for some time.

Just to give you an idea of the educational challenges I faced, I was diagnosed with the most common form of dyslexia, a broad term to describe a learning disability that hampers fluency or comprehension accuracy. Dyslexia, however, should not be confused with poor or inadequate reading instruction, which is often more likely the case. For me, it was real.

On a daily basis, it would often take me hours to do what a so-called normal child could do pretty quickly. It affected me socially, emotionally, and educationally.

I flourished in the one-on-one setting, but due to budget cuts in the early 1980s, the school I came to love was closed, and I was placed in Potomac Landing Elementary School. This school was a complete contrast to Harmony Hall. There was over-crowding, and I quickly got lost and fell through the cracks.

My parents worked hard to ensure that I was not left out or labeled in any way. They shared a story with me about a teacher who called me "retarded" because I learned slower and differently from the other children. My parents decided to hire a tutor who worked with me daily and never gave up on me. I attended occupational therapy classes where I was able to work on my motor skills, and I even signed up to play on the local soccer team.

Soccer was the best. I remember one early Saturday morning when I was about 5 years old, playing on my brother's soccer team. I was placed in the game and can recall being dreadfully nervous. Maybe that's why I embarrassed my brother by side-tackling another boy with the ball, and shooting it into my own net. That's one of the first memories I have of soccer. I was so young that I do not remember being embarrassed by the event, but I definitely learned a great deal about myself and realized I loved the sport.

Those were rough years for me. Kids can be cruel, and while I tried to be cool, I wasn't exactly what you would call one of the coolest kids in elementary school. I just did not fit in with certain cliques. Couple that with a learning disability and you can imagine why my self-esteem often took big hits.

Despite everything, I would say I had a pretty normal childhood in my early years because my parents did what they could to make my life as normal as possible. I went to Boy Scouts and other activities, but soccer was my main outlet to burn off any negative energy. It also gave me something to believe in, focus on, and taught me the meaning of being a part of a team.

I can recall times when I felt like I was the only one on the field because I had a sense of self when I got on the pitch. For those of you who may not know, the soccer field is called "the pitch". I actually became very skilled at it because I was determined and practiced a lot.

During this time, I was very fun-loving and always had a number of close friends. One of those friends, Michael, is still my best friend today. No matter what happened throughout my life and no matter how crazy the circumstance, he was always there with me.

My friend, Michael, is the ultimate deal maker. I can't remember when I first met him, but apparently he and I had a snowball fight where I was hit in the face with a snowball that had ice in it. My face was cut, so I ran down the street to get my brother Josh. When Josh arrived on the scene, Michael began to negotiate like a senator in committee. What was so astonishing is that he's the same way today, but considerably more sophisticated.

Michael would be the first to tell you about my greatest virtues and what a great guy I am. On the other hand, he'd also tell you things about me as a kid that will make you laugh and leave you shaking your head in disbelief. We grew up in a very racially integrated environment that was constantly changing around us. In the late 1970s, when my adoption was finalized, the county was becoming more diverse by the mid 1980s. I had all types of friends with different ethnic backgrounds. We called ourselves the United Nations Crew. Michael was African American; Jason was Guamanian; Jerome was African American; and my brother Josh was Caucasian. We grew up unconcerned about skin color, but many experiences to come, would show us that not everyone in society took this position.

We were always pretty easy-going kids, but we still had no problem mixing it up with kids who were ready to challenge us or were overly inquisitive about our background. More than anything though, we enjoyed ourselves and did what most young people did.

I had friends, but because of the incessant teasing, I managed to get into a number of fights in school. I just tried to fit in as best I could. By the time I got to the seventh grade, I tested at a fourth grade level. My parents searched hard to find me a school that would give me the more individualized attention I desperately needed.

They found a school in Laurel, Maryland, The Rineheart School. This school catered to special needs. At that time, I believe there were only about 150 students in the entire school. I can remember there only being about three kids in my math class, so I was definitely in a place where I could get the individual academic help I needed and could work on my socialization skills.

I excelled in school at that point because I believed in myself, and had an expectation that I could be great. It is true that young people will rise to the level of expectation, and because I wanted so desperately to succeed, I worked that much harder.

It was a difficult time, but my friendships helped. I was fortunate to have strong relationships with people, including family members. I was especially close to my brother Josh, but like most siblings, he and I used to fight like you would not believe.

I can recall many instances of the great rivalry between Josh and I where he let me know he was the boss and subsequently taught me the ropes of being a baby brother. When I think of those times now, I sit back and laugh because I would not have it any other way. Josh and I have had some very funny experiences and times with each other, but of course back then I probably did not think it was funny. I remember the day Josh introduced me to hockey by whacking me on the head with a hockey stick as he taught me the fundamentals of the game. I picked up the nearest thing closest to me while we played hockey in our garage and threw a matchbox car that was lying on the garage floor at his head. I sought payback, and yes I whacked him real good. We started to tussle, but with Josh and I, we were always looking for the next opportunity to show how we could get a leg up on the other person. You can probably tell that we both were very competitive and this played out through much of our youth. Another funny memory that comes to mind is the time when Josh really got me good while I was practicing soccer in the backyard. Josh and his friend were in his bedroom looking out at me as I ran back and forth. Josh and his friend opened the window very slowly and quietly, making sure I could not hear them. Josh then took aim and used my backside for target practice. I heard laughter, but was too focused on what I was doing to even care. Just as I was about to hit the ball one more time with my head, I felt a sharp pain. I saw my brother and his friend laughing in the window, and I immediately knew he had just shot me in the backside with his BB gun because I saw him pulling the gun back in through the window. I ran upstairs and tried to knock the door down to get to my brother, but he had locked me out. I spent several minutes doing falling dropkicks into the door. I wanted to take a piece out of Josh, as he just did with me. I was so determined to get to him, that I convinced myself I would get him back someday. This came true, as I repaid the deed many times over in the years to come.

These were just some of our altercations. For those of you who think that was just way too much, it's actually just the tip of the iceberg. Despite our disagreements and fights, we are two brothers that love each other unequivocally and unconditionally.

I can also recall a time when my Dad came home from work early because he wasn't feeling well. He told us not to wake him, but like most kids, we made noise anyway. My Dad is a big and imposing man, but he never really laid a hand on us. He truly is a gentle giant.

Anyway, me and Josh got into an altercation and were circling one another around the kitchen table when a chair or something toppled over and crashed to the floor. Before we knew it, we heard a loud thud and knew we had violated our dad's instructions and awakened him. He wasn't happy, and as we heard his loud, booming voice from upstairs, we quickly went from being adversaries to allies.

Josh and I had to find a way out of the house before Dad could get downstairs. Just seconds before, we were trying to rip each other's heads off, but now that it was clear that both of us were going to get it, we were quickly advocating for each other. We just wanted to survive.

Josh bolted out the side door to the garage, and I thought I was going to make it to the front door, but it wasn't to be. My Dad caught me and disciplined me good. I wasn't mad at Josh for bolting because our general rule was to save yourself.

I grew up in a close-knit community and us kids had a tendency to pick up strays, as in stray kids. Every time our parents they turned around, one of us was bringing someone else in and they would usually just nod, say hello, and act as if the kid, whoever he or she was, had always been there. That was part of the beauty of our lives. Growing up in a real community where people cared for one another was a gift, and it's something I want my son to experience.

Thankfully, he is living it, and I can honestly say it's working to his benefit. Oftentimes, children who do not have the experience of growing up in a loving environment find it difficult to cope. This can translate into destructive behavior in school, disrespect to their elders and no real concept of realistic future goals. They don't understand what intellectual and social freedom means beyond the already established lexicon that they may or may not have heard in school.

My friends and I are blessed to have been born into the families we have. I speak even for myself in this regard because, while I wasn't born into the Harrison family by blood, I am their son, and they are a family of strong values that cares about people, community, and education. My family continued to act on their beliefs to find me a school where I could excel.

I attended the Rinehart School for one year as a seventh grader, and the following year was enrolled at Riverdale Baptist School in Largo, Maryland. It was a pivotal year for me. At this religious-based school, I was introduced to spirituality and the idea that there is a being or a spirit out there with a higher order of love thinking, spirituality, and who or what God is. A seed was planted, and a foundation was laid in for my life.

Eighth grade would also prove to be pivotal. Prior to that, I looked at my siblings and did not feel any different from them or any other child. At times I would look in the mirror and realize that I did not physically look like them. I would often spend hours just looking at my features. It would baffle me, being a couple of shades darker than my siblings. I would wonder where whose physical characteristics did I have, whose nose,   chin, eyes, eyebrows, and lips did I have? I would point to each part of my face and would wonder who I looked like and whose facial reactions did I have. I would often practice different emotions in the mirror as though it was speaking back to me. I felt like the mirror could give me all the answers I was searching for. I wanted so bad just to fit in like the rest of my siblings. They knew their physical identity and I did not. I felt like that question would never be answered and this greatly affected my self-confidence. It was so very important to me to understand my traits and who I was. I was not concerned about whether or not I was attractive, or ugly, or how people or kids perceived me. I just wanted answers so badly.

Josh had red hair and freckles; John had blonde hair and blue eyes; and Heather had brown hair and blue eyes. Heather reminds me of the actress Demi Moore that I thought she shared some of the same physical characteristics. Even though I was still fairly unaware of differences in race, I was at a stage in my life when I began to wonder about my identity constantly as it was like a song that plays over and over again on the radio that you cannot escape.

I knew that I wasn't the Harrison's biological child, but the real questions of my birth and the circumstances surrounding it began to creep into my psyche, almost as if it was a call to action. It was impossible to shake. I had to know where I came from. It was like a dream I needed to pursue.

I often wondered about my birth mother and where she was. Was she married to my father and did they make just one bad decision in life by leaving me? Why did she leave me? Was I not good enough? Was she looking for me? Was she worried about me? Did she care whether or not I lived or died? Did she care whether or not I was hungry or safe? Then my thoughts would reverse, and I would become concerned about her well-being and what was happening in her life. I wanted to understand my story and situation.

This cycle fed on itself regularly and it would be a few decades before I would get any answers. In the meantime, I awoke each day and faced down my demons and issues. I was determined and confident that I was getting another step closer to becoming the man I was meant to be, never realizing how hard I would have to climb the mountain of answers to have some clarity. I hope you can see how my circumstances made it very easy for me to fall into periods of depression

This would happen from time to time, but because I had so much to do and was an energetic teenage boy, there were plenty of other pursuits that occupied my time and my thoughts. This would allow these periods to pass, but then, incidents would occur that would conjure up those feeling and thoughts once again.

I remember one day waiting for my brother to return home on the school bus. It was a cloudy day in the late 1980s, and as he was walking off the bus I said, "Josh, the fellas are ready to play some football." Josh did not look as if he wanted to play, and he seemed a bit shaken. I asked him what was wrong, and he replied,

"This stupid kid just said something so dumb to me." I asked him what he said.

Josh said, "As we were pulling up to the stop to let me off the bus, I was talking to this kid. I said I was excited to play football with my little brother this afternoon." Josh then pointed and said, "That's my brother standing right there." The kid looked out the school bus window at me standing at the bus stop and said, "What did your mother do have sex with the milk man?"

I was always ready to rumble, especially for my brother because I loved him so much. The funny thing is that I was such a skinny kid, but I was never scared to fight anyone, regardless of how much they towered over me. I relate it to a small dog always barking loudly at a dog twice its size.

Josh was so upset by this kid's actions and wanting to wail on him. Kids, as innocent as they can be, do not understand the hurt their words can cause and how damaging it can be to other children their age. As I became older, this began to ring so true.

Even though these things were happening in my life, I knew nothing about the home lives or families of most of my classmates, and they knew nothing about mine. On the outside, my actions were as normal as everyone else my age. While we were in school, it was about making good grades and friends. It was never about identifying and dealing with serious issues like adoption and feelings of abandonment, no matter how deeply rooted the feelings may be.

Many young people act out due to circumstances that many of the people around them are not aware of. This causes them to routinely end up in trouble spots, constantly needing a parent or guardian to bail them out until they find themselves at the wrong end of a police issued 9mm handgun, or in handcuffs on their way to jail. The hope is that it doesn't get to that point, but in far too many cases, it does. I had my share of rough days when I did not want to do this or that, but at least I had soccer and my family to keep me grounded.

Knowing that I wasn't the same as my brothers and sister, prompted me to ask my mother who I really was and what had happened to cause some of the problems I had. I basically wanted to know how I ended up with them. I soon came to find out that my parents were in the process of learning along with me.

Emotionally, I didn't handle things well and had a very quick temper. There were times when I would get in trouble in school because my coping skills were lacking. I wanted so desperately to understand what was going on with me and I felt that discovering my race was a big part of that.

I knew that I didn't look anything like the family that had adopted me, and I had to come to a point of acceptance. Still, it didn't make things right for me like I thought it would. To say that I was confused is an understatement. There were cultural issues that came up, and I began to understand them much better as I approached young adulthood. I was wrong. It wasn't finding my race that would free me, it was finding my identity.

One thing that would get me every time is the reaction we would get when my brother and I went to other neighborhoods to play. We would be introduced, first my brother and then me. The reactions and stares of the other kids were weird. Even weirder were the reactions of adults and the difference in those reactions based on race.

We'd go barreling into a house and be introduced to the parents of a Caucasian family, and they would literally sit there and stare, trying to figure it out, whereas African American families did not so much as bat an eye. The only thing African American parents would do is warn us not to break anything as we were playing around. This was the continuation of an education that my siblings and I received not only from my parents but from everyone around us.

Another issue, that I struggled with, was taking tests. I was never particularly proficient at taking standardized tests and the pressure would begin as soon as I sat down. I was always asked my race at the very beginning, and there was always a White, Black,

Hispanic, and Other box to choose from. I remember asking myself what is "Other" and did I classify as "Other"? I am not White, but my family is. Am I Black? Am I Hispanic? I didn't know, so I guess the safe bet is "Other", whatever that means.

Despite the deep issues I was dealing with, my friends and I did the normal things that kids did. We ran the streets, played football, soccer, and basketball, and enjoyed going to parties around the way. What I think was most distinctive about our crew was that we truly got a chance to be raised around all different types of ethnic backgrounds which allowed us to see the importance of different cultures and beliefs.

I'll admit it; I've always been fond of the ladies, so meeting girls was definitely one of my interests during that time as well. I remember when we were younger, we went to the mall, and a bunch of ladies gave me their numbers. My brother and friends asked me whether I knew them, and I told them that I did not. They stood off to the side and looked at me as if I lost my mind when I asked them if it happened to them too, as if that was something normal. They responded with a chuckle and said, "No."

Frustration was at its peak for me in high school. I was still struggling with questions about my identity and the bullying, racism, hatred and jealously from others made it even worse.

In June of 1989, I was entering ninth grade and enrolled in Frederick Douglass High School in Upper Marlboro, Maryland. I had been shuttled from school to school because of the adjustment and educational problems I had. My parents tried hard to find the right balance, along with the right type of school, so I could overcome some of my learning issues.

During this time, I experienced racial hostility from some of my peers but I have always been a believer in people. I didn't even think about race until I got older, and it became even more confusing to me as I entered high school. Josh and Heather were attending private school at Queen Anne High School in Upper Marlboro, MD. It was pretty much an entirely Caucasian school, and I remember my brother Josh getting teased because of the way he spoke.

One day, a kid in his grade began to talk about him. I do not want to repeat the racially charged words that this kid said to my brother, but they were very hurtful and mean. When my brother returned home, he told me that a kid at school said something terribly mean and cruel to him. He was angry because he was not used to such blatant racism. In our home environment, we did not judge people by the color of their skin but by their character. The only things that mattered were the fun we had with one another and how we bonded as friends.

It was around this time in my life that my brother began to open up about the racism he experienced as well. My brother heard and saw a lot of things through my adoption. He saw how neighbors treated my parents when I was a toddler and how we lost friends because they were a Caucasian family that had adopted a biracial baby. Throughout the years, this never stopped because there were always people who had no problem showing their arrogance and feelings of supremacy.

Ninth grade is when I began to really understand the issues between the races and how I fit into the mix or rather, how I didn't. At Frederick Douglass High School, it appeared to be approximately fifty percent African American and fifty percent Caucasian. Frederick Douglass High is also where I learned that I enjoyed music that spoke mainly to the African American experience. I felt that I was gaining a sense of identity.

I was doing what I could to pass, but I never actually applied myself enough to do my very best. I was routinely frustrated, overwhelmed and in need of direction. Learning disability aside, however, I know now that there were things I could've done to improve myself. I guess this happens as we grow older.

During this time in my life, I unfortunately faced a number of racially charged situations as well. This was all happening during a time in my life when I was still trying to figure out the basics of my background and who I was.

At this point, I didn't know for sure what my race was or who my biological parents were. Despite this, I still had to deal with people questioning and berating me and my background in ways that went completely against everything that my parents taught me.

The racial tension I experienced did not come from all of the students. I definitely had friends of all races who never questioned me or my racial background, and better yet, didn't care. Unfortunately, this was not my experience with everyone.

I can recall very vividly a Caucasian student, who I thought very highly of, calling me the "n-word" and "n-lover" because I gravitated toward African American females. This was particularly pivotal because there were some African American students who would tease me and call me "white boy" due to my very light skin and straight hair. I am not trying to water down the story, but I use "n-word" instead of that derogatory term because of how painful it is for me to this day. That word strikes a very negative chord for me and I have no desire to repeat it. Being called that term, especially by someone I thought so highly of, was one of my most hurtful moments in high school.

The word was used in a way that indicated the person making the statement felt superior to me. I was still trying to figure out who I was and what I did know about myself was garnering this reaction? It was difficult and confusing, to say the least.

I know that people would always wonder what my race was. Because of my appearance, it wasn't too much of a stretch for anyone to guess, but whenever they would see my father drop me off at school, I could tell that they were wondering. Without asking me, they would still manage to pigeon-hole me into whatever racial category they decided.

One day, there was a substitute teacher in my class, and we all know how students can be when there is a substitute. One of the students was trying to pick a fight with me because I was talking to a girl he liked. He started throwing things at my head and then proceeded to say, "I saw that honky drop you off. You don't know what you are. You look Mexican to me. If I were your biological parents, I would have left you too."

We began to fight. I punched him and slammed his head into the door. It may sound extreme but imagine being told these things in front of the entire class when you are already struggling with your identity. Both of us were suspended. I did not win all of my fights, but I did win this one. Regardless of the reasoning, I had lost this one mentally. I lost because I allowed my temper to get the better of me in this situation. My father used to talk to me a great deal about how I should not let the actions of others prevent me from being the bigger person.

When I was in the tenth grade, our family moved to a more "country" area of Upper Marlboro, Maryland. They bought an old farmhouse that was about two-hundred-years old and remodeled it. While it was an interesting, quiet, and very nice place, I missed the friends I grew up with. The house sat on a few acres of land and felt somewhat isolated. At the time, it was necessary because my father believed I would begin hanging around with the wrong people. Again, my parents were doing whatever they could to save me from myself.

This change was necessary, and the concept of change became a very significant part of my young life. At the time, I didn't understand the importance of change, physical and mental, in shaping who I am and my understanding of the world around me. My parents are in real estate, so it wasn't a stretch for me to see them busy working hard and showing me that being successful was hard work.

During this time, Prince George's County was becoming more and more sensitive to minorities, and there was clearly racial tension in the county. I can remember my brother taking me to my Aunt's house one day. I was scheduled to stay there for the night. It was the day of the Rodney King incident which sparked outrage and debate, not only in Los Angeles, but across the nation.

As we pulled into my aunt's neighborhood, we approached a stop sign, and then a speed bump. My brother was driving, and I was in the passenger seat. As my brother waited for a car coming from the other direction to stop, I noticed that some kids were beginning to walk toward the truck. I noticed them earlier, but they were just hanging out on the corner at the time.

They walked in front of the truck and began to hit it, shout expletives, and racial epithets toward my brother and me. These kids were just looking for trouble and I took real offense to their comments, especially the racial slurs. It was in the middle of the day, and despite my calm demeanor when I first arrived at my aunt's house, I was ready to rumble. What made this period in my life even worse is that I would get these types of reactions from both African American and Caucasian people.

The racial tension in the county all too often showed itself in the form of racial profiling. Too often, people think that because you don't look a certain way, there's something wrong or you are up to no good. The law has to protect citizens in the community but when it comes to protecting and serving, overzealous racial profiling is not the answer and in any case, should never occur—but it does.

I remember having an unfortunate experience with a sheriff that worked for the sheriff's department in the early 1990s. It was a summer evening in July 1991. It was within 60 days of the Rodney King incident and NWA songs were all over the radio. I was using a pay phone, and my friend was sitting and waiting in the car. I had on a sweat suit and was sporting a short hair cut, one that we would describe as an "even-steven" close cut.

I was looking at my pager, getting ready to call a friend to see if we could all hang out, when I turned my head toward the street. Immediately, I saw a sheriff's car pulling out of the drive thru at a Wendy's restaurant and the officer parked. I guess he was monitoring me, because I noticed he was staring at me. He rolled down the window of his cruiser and shouted, "Hey boy! Hey boy. Stop slinging rocks and get off that phone." All I could immediately think was, what did he just say to me?

This was my first encounter with the law. It felt like a movie, but it was not. All I was doing was speaking to a girl on the phone. He said, "Hang up that phone now." I obliged and did not want to give the officer any problems. I know how that can turn out. I responded, "yes, sir" to his orders, and he then told me to walk toward him and show him my ID. I was so nervous, because I believed this officer was looking for me to disrespect him.

I walked toward the vehicle, and that's when he uttered the words, "get on your face 'n-word'." This was the second time I had been called this word in a two-month period. All I could feel was the back of a gun barrel pressed against my head with force. I was terrified, afraid, and every other word that exemplifies fear. Shaking like a leaf, in that moment, I knew that this racist officer had the power to take my life or do whatever he wanted. It was numbing to say the least. I had always suffered through nightmares on a regular basis, because of other issues that I was dealing with, and now this. To have an officer of the law abuse his power just to terrify me made these nightmares real.

I was lying on my face with the rough edges of concrete pressed against my face, and the physical discomfort was overwhelming. This officer was an overweight Caucasian man with blond hair and a mustache. He took my wallet and then positioned me in the upright position. I sat on the curb and he went back to his vehicle and did a check to see if I was in the system.

I checked out clean and then he said, "Hey, you can go kid; you're clean." He then threw my wallet on my lap, walked back to his cruiser and pulled off. I remember feeling so angry and scared all balled up into one giant emotion.

I told my father about this and I thought he would be mad at me but instead, he was angrier about the fact that it had happened to me. My father took me to the precinct to find the officer who had done this. When we found him, we realized that he was a sheriff who had done some evictions for my father. He never explained his actions, and I remember him looking stunned and shocked that I was my father's son. The situation was resolved with an apology and an understanding that nothing like that would ever happen again, but I often wondered what would have happened had my father not been who he was.

What if my father had not known the officer? Would this circumstance have ended with an apology? Would there have been any resolution? Unfortunately, this scenario plays out all too often between minorities and law enforcement officers, and typically doesn't end so amicably.

To shed light on this topic, I remember my father sharing stories about his father and what past generations had to deal with as the fight for racial equality raged on. My father began to convey the lessons that my grandfather shared with him.

My grandfather was a truck driver when he returned home from WWII, a member of the Greatest Generation. I believe he drove tanks in Europe, a perilous job at any time in history, but he did it fighting the Nazi's. When he returned home things hadn't changed much in America, especially regarding race. Jim Crow Laws were paralyzing and crippling the country, but my grandfather was different from a lot of his peers.

Proof of this came one night at a truck stop while he and some of his buddies were having coffee and chatting. During that time, the laws were so restrictive that everything, including truck stops, was segregated. Out of the night, came a truck that was clearly disabled and stopped in front of the area where my grandpa was. He was surprised to see an African American man hop out of the cab of the truck.

The man began to explain that he knew he wasn't supposed to be there, but all he wanted was to get back home to his family. My grandfather took pity on the man. He took a look at the truck to see if he could make it go, but helping hands or not, it was still the South, which was not the friendliest place for an African American man, especially late at night.

Shortly after being noticed, a group of Caucasian truckers came spilling out of the truck stop, and the African American man began to fear for his life. He was so fearful that when my grandfather told him to start the truck after he had finished working on it that he gunned the engine nearly knocking my grandfather to the ground. My grandfather got up and shouted at the man, causing others to come over and do the same.

My grandfather climbed up to the cab to see what the man's problem was. When he got up to the cab, my grandfather could clearly see a deeply concentrated fear. He helped a man who, for those days, knew he was in the wrong place.

My grandfather assumed that he would be happy with the assistance, so he was surprised to find that the man was fearful---but he had good reason for such fear. An African American man at a "Whites only" truck stop somewhere in the South was a recipe for a disappearance. Realizing the fear in his eyes, my grandfather jumped off of the truck and watched the man drive off.

I don't tell the story nearly as well as my Dad, but you get the idea. My grandfather learned quite a lesson that night. He subsequently taught it to my Dad, who then taught it to me, and I have now taught it to my son. Rev. Dr. Martin Luther King, Jr. spoke of judging a man by the content of his character and not the color of his skin. My family has tried to live up to this standard.

My dad owned and operated real estate offices all over Prince George's County for over 40 years. He always hired people, regardless of race, in leadership positions to work for and with him. He raised us to believe that if you work hard, do the right thing, and let your actions speak for themselves, doors will open up for you in life. My parents tried to protect us from the racial elements of the world, and showed us that the only thing that mattered was the power of love. We realized, however, that the rest of the world did not always see things this way.

As I grew older and more mature, I began to appreciate the differences as well as the commonalities between the cultures I shared. I knew that there was something special and unique about everything around me, but my interest in knowing more about my birth parents continued to grow stronger and stronger.

While other students were preparing for college and considering who and what they would be in life, all I could think of was finding her--finding my birthmother. The struggles I faced all through school signaled to me that college was not going to be an option. Say what you will about working hard, trying, and all of that, but I knew it just wasn't for me.

My parents also went through some ugly moments as a result of having me in their home. When they adopted me, they lost friends because of things that had been said about me and their care for me. I would thank them for this but thanking them for loving me seems ridiculous. It's what true parents seem to do naturally.

My parents were not crusaders from the Civil Rights Movement seeking to right all of the social ills of the time, but they were loving and caring parents who just wanted to open their home to a child that needed it. They had their share of challenges raising me, but no one and nothing was going to get in the way of their love for me. I appreciate them every day for that.

It takes time to plant seeds of equality and even more time to see the cultivation of those seeds turn into plants of hope. Upon graduating high school in June of 1993, I was introduced to the real world. Life truly started happening. Since I didn't go to college and bounced from job to job for a few years, my dad suggested I learn a trade.

Within four years of my graduation, I had a son and was really trying to find my way. My parents were always right there to ensure that I would be the best parent I could be. I was also fortunate to have maintained a good relationship with my son's mother in spite of our personal relationship having gone awry.

I had just about every job you can imagine---fast food, carpet cleaning, working at the mall, selling alarm systems---you name it, I did it. It was all about an honest day's work, so I could take care of myself and my son. I decided to take my father's advice, and pursued plumbing. I became an apprentice plumber and learned the craft well. I enjoyed it because I worked well with my hands and ultimately, became a service plumber.

I entered my young adult years, and was trying to embrace my new career, and being a new father. My son was about two years old, and I realized there was something missing in my life—soccer. I was so in love with the sport, and even though I dreamed of being a professional soccer player, I soon realized it wasn't to be and started to think about how I could fill this void.

I thought about my son and whether or not he would like soccer, or any sport. I began to place a soccer ball at his feet at the age of two. He would just run around kicking the ball and smiling. I said to myself, I think I have a little soccer player, and smiled from ear to ear.

Most fathers dream of coaching their son, especially in a sport that they love. My opportunity came in the spring of 1999 in Bowie, Maryland. My son Jerrell, was playing for the South Bowie Sharks with sixteen other kids, and I was the head coach. I was very nervous, but was looking forward to teaching the sport. I also wanted to teach the importance of teamwork in everyday life situations.

My first year was a rough one because I had to teach them how to play as a team. I made my expectations on and off the field clear. Good grades were a must, and I told them to expect that we would win several championships. The first year we lost about four games and were a sub five hundred team. I was not happy with those results because I love to win. It's not always about talent it's about belief. You can have all the talent in the world, but if you don't have heart then you cannot win.

The second year, I noticed the kids where excelling. They had all the tricks down and could shoot the ball, so I had a long talk with myself about how we could get better. I won't go into all of the techniques but needless to say, I like to win, and we practiced like we expected to win.

One of my techniques was to have the players practice with ankle weights. When it was game time, we began to fly like the wind, kicking and shooting with power. No one could match our intensity, and with my brass style of coaching, we destroyed teams for the next seven years.

We won three county championships, and went to five more championships that we lost in a penalty shoot out. My team's record over an eight year period was 59 wins and only 8 losses. More than the wins, I really enjoyed teaching the boy's about life, overcoming adversity and following your heart.

My son had the opportunity to learn the sport I fell in love with, and became an even more dominant soccer player than I was. As the boys approached the age of thirteen, I decided to resign and give them the opportunity to learn the sport from someone else. I believed that I had taken them as far as I could, and now it was time for them to grow beyond what I could teach them. Half of that team now plays soccer in high schools all across Prince George's County. That makes me very proud. My son Jerrell is currently starting and one of the leading scorers on his team today. That makes me even prouder.

Coaching my son gave me a sense of belonging, because I was now doing something for my son that had been done for me. It's interesting how life tends to come full circle if you're around long enough to really see and experience it.

I knew I needed to start dating. I found that each time I would do so, there still seemed to be a huge hole in my heart. It was pretty obvious that something was terribly wrong with me, and it manifested itself in my relationships with women. There would be a few dates, and just like that, it would be over.

I don't want to place the blame on the women I dated for the demise of these relationships because it was clear that I was the cause. This goes way beyond the commonly used phrase, "it's not you, it's me". This was about my trust issues and my inability or unwillingness to let people in. It really was me, and I had to make myself whole before I could begin to look at anyone else.

I would not allow people to get very close to me. These intimacy and trust issues prevented the furtherance of any personal relationships. Opening up to people became a real challenge. An empty space cannot be filled by simply adding anything or anyone. In fact, adding certain things and people, can make it worse.

My life had become little more than going through the motions, all the while trying to figure out who I really was and where I came from.

I wanted to understand my story and situation. I wanted to know who my birthmother was. It was a question I thought about daily. I thought about the color of her skin and the scent of her hair. I wanted to know her story and be able to wrap my arms around the whole situation. This biggest question I had was why?

The question haunted me the older I got. I knew that the only way to move forward was to begin my search for my birthmother. It was the only way that I could put the pieces to this confusing puzzle together, and get on with my life. I believe in my heart that the subsequent events shaped the rest of my life.

4

The Search

It was shortly before 9/11 when my search officially began. I went to Children's Hospital in Washington, DC and requested my medical records. My Mom told me what my birth name was and once I received the records, I learned that my birth mother's name was Jody. That's it, no middle or last name. Just Jody.

I then went to the district courthouse, paid to have the seal removed from my adoption records, and found a social worker willing to work with me. By 2004, the social worker had been working on the case for about a year, when I heard from my brother, Josh. I was at a Jiffy Lube getting the oil changed in my car, when the call came in.

I remember sitting in there for a while and hearing my brother tell me that the social worker had found my mother. I felt a little anxious because I remembered my father telling me to be careful about opening doors until I was prepared to face what was behind them. It can and typically does affect the people around you, both positively and negatively.

The feeling of expectation was overwhelming and I remember feeling afraid of walking through that door of knowledge and yet, uncertainty. I sat outside the Jiffy Lube on the curb and cried. I cried because I was relieved that she had been found, but I also regretted that so many years had passed. I wasn't sure who or what she was going to be or if she even wanted to be bothered with seeing me.

I knew one way or the other, good or bad, that something was going to come of this revelation. It was three days before Mother's Day and my anxiety level was at a fever pitch. I felt that I was betraying my parents because of all they had done for me, and I was concerned about how would they feel. I spent a great deal of time having conversations with myself in an attempt to prepare for what those first moments might be like. The fact is that I could never prepare myself. This was going to be a pivotal, life changing moment, regardless of the outcome.

During the search I always thought about who she was. It was constantly on my mind. I wanted to know the story of who I was, and I would constantly dream about it. Despite thinking about it for years, I still felt extremely overwhelmed when I finally found her. What was I going to say to her? I just really could not believe that this was happening.

I wondered if I would be cold and distant the first time I heard her voice. I didn't want her to feel overwhelmed or awkward, but I knew that no matter how much I tried to prepare, it was going to be an emotionally awkward moment for both of us. I kept asking myself if I was really ready to deal with this. If I didn't know anything else, I knew that after I made this phone call, my life would be forever changed. That thought alone was a lot to process.

Finally, I just picked up the phone and started to dial the ten digit phone number. I held the last number down for what seemed like forever, in one last attempt to get ready for the conversation. The phone rang three times when a woman picked up on the other end and said "Hello".

"Hello is Jody in?" I replied, voice cracking.

"This is Jody," the voice replied.

"Please excuse me for a moment, but I don't think you are aware of who you are speaking with," I said in a calm, but nervous voice.

"Well, who is this?" she asked.

I replied, "This is your birth son Sydney Jerome Harrison. "OH MY GOD," she said, after a second or two of dead silence. "Who is this again?" I repeated myself and then she began to cry for a long time. "I am so sorry," she said. "The only time I thought I would be able to hear your voice or be with you again, was in heaven. I have prayed for this day to happen."

"I am sorry," she repeated several times, with her voice too weak to understand at times.

I let her know that it is a good day because we were both alive and well. The phone call lasted about two hours, and I didn't know how or what to feel. This was really just too much for my brain to comprehend, so I spent most of the time listening to her and letting her explain things in her own way.

She explained that she was crying because she had carried so much guilt for what happened. My birthmother was not in a good place, and I was crushed. She informed me that she had been under the influence of drugs for some time and over the years had been in a series of bad, abusive relationships with men.

Having married a few times, unsuccessfully, she was clearly overwhelmed with life. We decided to meet. I arranged our meeting at a local restaurant, because I thought a place that had food and a pretty good atmosphere would be a good idea. I also asked that she bring her strongest supporters, because I knew that this would be a difficult meeting for both of us. After all of the emotional torment we had both been through prior to meeting, we were finally going to see one another face-to-face.

I arrived a little late to the meeting and brought several people with me including my best male friend, my best female friend and one of my brothers. I arrived late because I knew my birthmother would be traveling from Pennsylvania to Maryland, and I wanted her to get comfortable with her surroundings before meeting me. I walked in, saw her, and knew who she was right away. She was in tears and looked right at me. My knees were shaking as I walked toward her. My hands were clammy and my mouth was dry.

When I looked into my birthmother's eyes, I could immediately see myself. Everything from my face, lips, eyes and even my quirky laugh, I could now see in her.

It struck me as quite an interesting dynamic that I met her on my adoptive mother's birthday. On the birthday of the woman who nurtured and cared for me my entire life, there I was, standing face-to-face with the woman who birthed me and left me alone in the hospital. To say it was a wonderfully strange day is a serious understatement. I had a series of out of body experiences and felt as though I would pass out at times during the meeting.

It was like I was completely outside of myself. Seeing her in person after wondering and imagining who she was for so long, was a surreal yet perfectly normal moment. Externally, it was normal because I am a people person and I treated this occasion as though I were just meeting another person. Internally, however, I was numb, nervous, anxious, excited, and confused.

I shared my life with my birthmother and brought her up to speed on what my life was like growing up. I am sure that I forgot some things, because we were trying to keep the moment as light as possible. This was our first meeting and I didn't want it to be too overwhelming. My feelings were rolling like an earthquake that rocked me to the core. There she was, the woman who gave birth to me, and the last time we laid eyes on each other was decades ago.

I was hard-pressed to get answers to questions that I had been wondering about my entire life. She had gotten her answers the moment she saw me. She knew I was alive, had a job, a son of my own and had become a productive member of society. She told me that she was seated at her kitchen table when she learned that I had found her. Her niece came over to her home and broke the news. Jody had been going through a deep depression prior to getting that news. Hearing it nearly sent her over the edge. I made her go through a lot of emotions that hadn't been dealt with for a long time. I remember her telling me that I was her dirty little secret for a long time. No one believed her, and now she was being confronted with her past all over again.

Filling in the gaps a bit, the social worker found an old tax record involving some property that one of Jody's relatives had sold. The people that bought the house knew my birthmother's mother. When a call was made to the house, her niece took the call and that's basically how the ball got rolling and Jody found out I was looking for her.

My birthmother got no support from her family during this time, which was not atypical for her at all. She had lived her entire life searching for love and acceptance only to have people repeatedly turn their backs and hurt her, so the lack of support was not unexpected. That was not an easy thing to hear, because it made me feel guilty for harboring ill feelings toward her.

She went on to tell me that she knew I was not going to be proud of her and that she had no good news to share with me.

For me to say I wasn't in some way disappointed would be a half-truth. My expectations had been dashed, and I was really judgmental toward her. I didn't like what I saw. I expected to see someone who had made really bad decisions in the past but was now on top of the world, but this was far from the case. She was still struggling with her drug use, among other issues. I know that it was unrealistic and in some ways, unfair to have such high expectations, but I think it's pretty normal to create an ideal of your mother in your mind, especially if you have never met her.

I remember being very polite, giving her a hug, and being respectful, despite some of the underlying pain I felt. The thing that blew me away and really surprised me about that day was the people in the restaurant who had gathered with us to witness this moment. They all stood up, clapped, and then came over to shake my hand. It was far from the sensationalized first meetings you'd see on a talk show because this was truly real, and there were no TV cameras to record the event and promote unnecessary drama.

Despite the meeting, I knew it was going to take time to build a relationship with her. I also drew a line in the sand that some may not agree with, but I needed to do it for my own sanity, because it was honestly how I felt. I tried to explain to my birthmother, as sensitively as I could, that while she was indeed my birthmother, she could never be my mother because I already have one.

I explained to her that, in the beginning, I needed to make sure I showed respect for my mother, who raised me, clothed me, nurtured me, and brought me back to health. The love of family was my mother. I will be forever grateful to my birthmother for giving me life, but we didn't need to worry about having a mother and son relationship. We needed to learn each other and how to become friends first.

I only have one mother and that's Mrs. Harrison. It may sound harsh, but I had to be honest about my feelings. In my view, it was the right thing to do at the time. I have endured the pain and the curiosity that felt like a lifetime, to meet my birthmother. I also had to practically move heaven and earth to find her. She didn't look for me, and that still bothered me. I thank her for giving me life, I thank her for not having an abortion, but I couldn't yet see my way clear to truly forgiving her. Forgiveness was a process that I knew I would have to endure and work hard to understand.

The figurative road I walked, searching for and subsequently finding my birthmother, was a treacherous one. After that first meeting, I shut down. My expectations were so high, and I believed they hadn't been met. It was very difficult to deal with, so I didn't speak to her for another year. I knew she was reaching out to me, but it wasn't just about her.

I had grown weary of my own issues and wanted life to get back to normal. I was fooling myself. Like my father said, once you open the door, you have to be prepared to deal with what's there. Closing the door and forgetting what was behind it was not an option.

I immediately got closer to my family because I felt that I had betrayed them for my own version of thirty pieces of silver. I thrust myself into the family business of real estate and shortly after getting into the business, the real estate market was collapsing. I found myself trying to navigate my way through that, along with the other issues I was dealing with. I basically felt like I was back to square one. I was trying to move on without dealing with the underlying issues I had with my birthmother.

To say my relationships with my birthmother and with my family were confusing would be an understatement. I had very conflicting emotions as I navigated these unchartered waters. I deeply loved my family and just hoped they could understand what I was going through. More importantly, I needed them to know why it was so important that I go through this journey.

Emotionally, I was still trying to deal with everything that happened after meeting my mother when my thoughts turned to my birthfather and who he was. The man my birthmother was with at the time of my birth signed the birth certificate, but was not my birth father. Upon learning the sordid details of the sadistic attack on my birthmother at his hands, I abandoned any thoughts or feelings I had about him or knowing who he was. What made perfect sense to me was that any man who would beat a woman and force himself on her was no father of mine. To me, the true definition of fatherhood was the man who had taught me all of my life lessons, my father.

One thing I knew is that I couldn't continue to carry around the burden of hurt, anger, and mistrust if I was going to find my center and the essence of my life-force. The Chinese speak of the Qi (pronounced chee) which is frequently translated into "life-force" or energy-flow. I was beyond tears, pain, and regret. It was time to start building, but what and how?

I spent so much time enduring the burden I was carrying, that I had placed a large part of my life on hold. In order to move on, I needed to know and accept the truth about everything. With the newly found knowledge of my past, I realized I had an opportunity to make more of my situation and the responsibility to help others in the process.

While the physical search was over, the emotional search was just beginning. I set out to discover who I was as a person and as a man. In conversations with friends and family, I was a pretty decent person by all accounts. That was certainly not to toot my own horn. I just want to openly acknowledge that regardless of what happened to me at my birth and throughout my youth, I am a man now and am tasked with certain responsibilities that I could not ignore.

As life continued, I decided that I needed to stop being so serious and sensitive all the time. I knew that I would never be a completely carefree kind of guy, but I did know how to relax and have fun, so I did whenever I got the opportunity.

It seemed like there were women everywhere, and as a young man in my early thirties, I definitely had taken notice. I decided not to allow any opportunity to go to waste, especially when it came to meeting someone special. I wouldn't call myself a ladies' man, like some of my friends, but I definitely was not shy about speaking to women and going out with them. I was in search of my soul mate.

I can recall several times being out with friends having a good time, and as usual, looking for ladies. I would marvel at how good life was becoming for me. My story, much like other's stories, had its challenging periods, but I felt like I was in a very good place. I planned to take full advantage of the good place I was in.

One evening my friends and I went to a bar not too far away from home. We decided to have some drinks and get something to eat. As I got dressed to leave, I was trying to figure out whether or not I had on the appropriate attire for where we were going. I had seen the place dozens of times but had never actually been inside. I settled on a pair of jeans and a button up Redskins polo shirt.

I arrived well before my friends, but this was not unusual. I could count on one hand how often they showed up on time for a social event. Maybe I was a stickler for time, but I liked to be prepared for whatever was coming my way. This turned out to be a good thing that night, because in a flash I felt someone staring at me. It wasn't the kind of stare that suggested something was wrong, i.e. my zipper being open, but something else.

Have you ever had the feeling that you were being watched, and every move and gesture was being tracked by someone? That's what I felt. The hairs on my face were standing up, and I turned to see who was there. I literally almost dropped the drink I ordered.

I couldn't believe it. There she was. Everything I had ever wanted in a woman. She was average height, perfectly proportioned, and had a smile that almost blinded me. She put out her hand and introduced herself. I will simply call her Monica.

Monica and I spent the next few moments smiling and checking each other out. I could feel her friends in the background watching our body language, but my focus was squarely on her. Not more than a few minutes had passed when I heard voices behind me. It was my friends arriving. The light-hearted moment I was sharing with Monica was slightly interrupted, but thankfully my friends are quite intuitive and recognized they were witnessing something special. They simply greeted me, told me where they would be, and walked away.

As she and I talked and nibbled on finger food, I thought about all I had been through, but not in a negative way. My life had turned around, and I found myself happy and hopeful about the opportunity of something special happening. Before we knew it, we were the only two people left in the place. Our friends had long left and we weren't even sure when. I'm sure we said our goodbyes to them and just lost track of time.

We finally left, and I walked Monica to her car. Neither one of us really wanted to leave, so we stood there talking even longer. We laughed about our friends leaving us and promised to keep in touch.

Monica and I began dating in earnest not too long after I met Jody, my birthmother. I spoke with Monica about my life and told her my story. She also told me about her life. She was a doctor and seemed very ambitious and successful. She seemed to be into me as much as I was into her. It was the first time in recent memory I had been so attached to someone outside of my son's mother and of course, my family. I wanted very much for us to grow together and make it permanent.

It was not very long after we began our relationship that I began to really open up to her and share my deepest feelings, hopes, and fears, and she reciprocated. Whatever it was that had been holding me back from sharing myself and my life with someone, was quickly drifting away. I was feeling new emotions and the excitement of all that was happening to me.

Monica had become as significant to me as my son, my family, and strangely, my birthmother too. Though each person's significance in my life was for different reasons, they all were critical. I include Monica in that group, because she was more than just a date, she was the woman that I was falling in love. I could see myself sharing my life with her. So, I guess it made sense to me that bonding with her so quickly felt so…right.

What I enjoyed most about Monica was her caring ways. She took the time to know me and was truly interested in getting to know me as a person. She challenged me, and I recall that moment in our relationship when my love for her really grew. She said, "Sydney, why will you not let me love you? Do you think you are not good enough to love? You are. You are great person with a huge heart." She said it so poetically, and I truly believed she meant it at that time.

She had a smile that would light up a room, and beautiful eyes. She too introduced me to the church and most importantly, to God. I went with her to church and bible study regularly. Soon I was praying, worshipping, and fellowshipping with her. She truly had a heart for God and really instilled that any man that wanted to be with her had to have his own relationship with God. He couldn't just say it; he had to show it through his actions and footsteps.

Everybody knows that relationships have what some term a "honeymoon period". In any relationship, whether personal, professional, or political, things are smooth, easy, and non-threatening during the "honeymoon period". The problem is that the "honeymoon period" always ends, and when it does, it can be stormy and downright nasty. You never see it coming.

A buddy of mine once said that the aftermath of the honeymoon will tell you what you really think and feel about a person. He was right, because the honeymoon was over and my feelings for Monica and her feelings for me were really being tested.

Like any other couple, we argued about things most people argue about--money, politics, religion, family, and friends. In our case, money became a poignant topic. During a period in our relationship, Monica paid for a lot of our activities. I was making the transition from being a plumber to becoming a real estate professional, and it was tough, especially financially. I had to pay for licensing and other things associated with my career transition, and it took a toll on me financially.

When you start something new in earnest, you usually take a hit in another area. In my case, it was my relationship. I had less and less disposable income, and it was a problem. At this point, I was basically just trying to live.

Monica, on the other hand, had a steady income thanks to her educational pursuits and a great job. I paid for things when I could, but her frustration with having to pay more than not suddenly turned sour. What began as a positive and potentially life-changing relationship had turned into more drama, but at least it was drama that we tried to maintain some level of control over.

The arguments never really turned nasty. We really did try hard to hold on to each other in spite of the obvious difficulties we were having. During this time, we were essentially playing house. I would stay with her occasionally, and as time went on, it began to weigh on her spirit. She believed that men and women should be married or engaged before living together. We were neither, and we didn't seem to be moving in that direction.

It was just a thought at the time, but I also began to notice her eyes wandering, specifically in the direction of other men. I was no longer what she wanted, and as far as I was concerned at the time, probably never was.

I have to admit that I am far from a gym rat and had never really put too much energy into maintaining six-pack abs and powerful biceps. I felt that Monica was into those qualities in a mate. I was just a regular guy that fell in love and wanted to be happy. Though I am not completely sure what Monica wanted in a man, it was becoming clearer and clearer to me that I wasn't it. As you could probably guess, it wasn't a particularly good feeling.

It was about a year and a half into the relationship and there were times when we would let days, even weeks, pass with scarce to no communication. I began to feel as if I didn't even have a girlfriend. The distance was made even greater by the fact that there were times when she was on call and legitimately could not see or had time to talk to me. This was obviously beyond her control, but it exacerbated the situation because of the distance we were already experiencing, separate and apart from her job.

My birthday was approaching and Monica phoned to tell me she was going to take me out. I was happy and had high hopes this would be a turning point for us. Despite my friend's theory on relationships and the "honeymoon period", I was thinking that just maybe we would be the exception. I'm not really sure why, but for me, hope always sprang eternal.

I went to meet her at the restaurant because she would be headed there straight from work. My heart skipped a beat as she walked in promptly at seven fifteen. I was already seated at the bar. She came over and greeted me with the sweetest kiss, and I breathed a sigh of relief. I felt she did still love me and wanted to make sure my birthday was special.

Monica and I were seated, and the server brought over the menus. Our conversation was flowing almost as if nothing had ever been wrong. Just as the drinks were arriving, she told me she needed to talk to me. Before she did, I inquired about the holidays because we had spent Thanksgiving, Christmas, and the New Year together, so I was looking forward to the same that year. Monica breathed deeply, took a sip of her drink, lifted her head, and looked at me. I knew something was up, because she didn't respond right away.

When she finally did, she told me her brother was having Thanksgiving at his house and that she would likely be there. She also said she was going out of town for Christmas. There was no mention of me or us in any of those plans, so I pretty much figured out what was going on. I immediately began preparing myself to hear the worst, but I didn't have nearly enough time.

Monica said that she felt horrible doing this on my birthday, but the words she spoke were like a stone to my heart. She said:

> "As I look at you and think about this relationship, I realize I can find someone better, who's bringing the same thing or better than I am to the table. I feel like being with you is like settling for less than the best. She then followed with, you're a really smart guy, and I know and you know you can do better, but you're just...not. So...I think it's best we just go our separate ways."

I know this may sound overly dramatic but I was kind of hoping she'd pull out a syringe of some lethal drug and jab it into my neck. As far as I was concerned living through that moment, and hearing those words come out of the mouth of the woman I loved was far worse.

I sat there in disbelief as the server brought our food with a huge smile on his face and asked if we needed anything else. Of course I did not respond. I felt like I had just been stabbed in the heart. The food, which was steaming in front of me, suddenly made me sick, and I immediately excused myself to the men's room and vomited. I'm not sure what I said to myself out loud while standing over the toilet, but I know a few foul words came out. This was not at all how I expected the evening to go, and I was pretty upset, to say the least.

As I stood up and went to wash my hands and face, I looked in the mirror and tried to get myself together. I tried to prepare myself and told myself there was no way I would let her see me crying. I didn't want her to think that she had that much control over my life or even the situation.

By the time I returned to the table, she had picked up her fork but was playing in her food and not eating. Her face was flushed, and she looked as though she had been crying. To say the silence was deafening and awkward would be an understatement, because we didn't say another word to each other for the rest of the evening. We just sat there as our food turned as cold as our emotions.

Just imagine where I was, what I heard and what I was going through at that moment. It seems horrible but, strangely enough, the news wasn't as catastrophic as I had initially feared. I needed to be real with myself. I saw it coming, and if I didn't, it probably was because I didn't want to. I liken it to a boxer who throws a punch and is met by a counterpunch that knocks him to the ground, dazed and confused. I was certainly down on the canvas, but I wasn't out. I knew a punch might hit me, and I was just resting as the ref counted. I knew I needed to stand up, shake it off, and finish as strongly as I could.

I took my hands and started to feel my face, arms, and legs. I was still alive. I suddenly broke into hysterical laughter, so much so, that she laughed a little too. I knew I was all right at that point and was determined not to show any weakness whatsoever. She needed to see me standing up and not lying down defeated, though I knew it would be a different scenario when I arrived home alone

Walking Monica to her car, uneaten food boxed and in hand, I hugged her and wished her well. She did the same. As she drove away, the tears began to fall as her taillights dimmed in the quieting distance.

Once I got home, I let it all out and became violently angry. My anger and despair was not so much about the act of breaking up as much as it was about what she said to me. I felt humiliated, emasculated, and ashamed. From my perspective, she had taken every ounce of self-esteem I had and told me I was nothing.

We both had issues we were dealing with, and maybe the only way to deal with them from her end was to just end the relationship. Sometimes we just get into relationships that are not necessarily good for us, and I didn't know what else she may have been dealing with that I didn't know about.

Despite the break-up, time didn't stop, and one thing I did know was that I needed to get myself together and think about what I was going to do with my life. As I stood in my mirror, as I had several times before, I thought about the significance of September 17th.

Though it was late at night, it was still my birthday. It was supposed to be one of the happiest days of the year for me, but all that happened was for the second time in my life, I had been left alone by someone who was supposed to love me.

All of this made me begin to wonder what God was trying to tell me and what I was supposed to learn from this experience. Some may say that it is a coincidence that these events happened on the same day, but I don't believe that. Everything happens for a reason and in this case, two of the people that were supposed to care the most about me, left. It left me feeling rejected...like I just couldn't cut the mustard.

I entered the therapist's office for the first time in years, and she looked at me with a concerned look on her face, and said, "How have you been Sydney?" This was not a good time. I was dealing with one of the hugest heartbreaks I had ever endured, and it was because, as a thirty two year old man, I fell in love for the first time. This was another failed relationship. I had been through them before, but this one really crushed me and crippled my ego, heart, mind, and soul. The feeling of heartbreak sucks, and all I could do was ask myself why?

Even though I had all of these emotions, I simply replied, "I have seen better days." She began to ask about my life and what had changed. As I spoke about finding my birthmother, she said, "You are a product of a rape?" She was silent and then said, "Wow Sydney, what else did you learn." I went on to explain that my birthmother used drugs and was a young teenager when she had me.

She then replied, "Sydney, I am sorry to hear that, but do you know what is beautiful about today and this situation?" I asked her, "what?" and she said, "you have the chance to pick up your broken heart that's in a million pieces and really learn one by one what fills your heart, what is the greatness that is in you and, what you have to do to become better than you were before. This process is hard, grueling, and takes commitment, but you must deal with it one day at a time."

She told me that we would start by doing some hands on things. She handed me a book to read. She told me to take my time chapter by chapter, identifying with the writer and determining how many things I had in common with this person. That sounded like something I could do. Then, she asked me to express how I felt at that moment. Did I feel nervous, anxious, or did I feel like I was doing the right thing by coming in for the session?

I basically told her that I was taking the first step in "fixing myself", but I was overwhelmed because I didn't know where to start. She started with an exercise. She told me to ask myself this question: "When you are upset about certain things that happen in your life, do you feel like you are going to explode or implode?" She asked me to give a rating from 1-5.

She then began to ask me questions about Monica, my family, and my birth family. She asked what my birthmother told me about my conception and how I felt about being a product of a rape. Did I feel like I wanted to implode or explode? I answered "implode".

She then asked me how I felt about suffering from emotional intimacy issues and how I felt about the things Monica said that hurt me. You can see the nature of the questions and how they were challenging my thought patterns and feelings. In case you couldn't guess, the answer to all the questions she asked was "implode".

For clarification, to implode means to let your temper flare inside of you. Holding everything in without release is not good for your body, mind, or spirit. To explode is to verbally let everything out. Done the right way, exploding can be a healthy expression with a responsible response.

She began to say, "Sydney it's okay. You have to release your frustrations. It's okay to express how you feel about everything that has happened to you. Anyone would be frustrated and angry in your situation."

I listened intently to the effective ways to simmer the fire that was in me and turn it into something positive. She let me know that we would have to talk about a lot of this and that it would take time, but if we practiced certain exercises, we would be able to effectively work through my feelings and find peace. But, it would require work...a lot of work. We began by discussing the issues I was experiencing with abandonment and rejection and how to make sense of it all.

She later conveyed to me that I must surround myself with people who cared and were positive. She began to explain how we as humans are like sponges that get saturated with the pressures of life. We tend to let other people's issues weigh us down without even realizing it.

When a sponge becomes saturated with water, you must wring it out, or it will become soggy and wet, tearing down the fabric of the sponge, causing it to be weathered and less useful.

This is the same with our lives. We must remove the saturation created by the negativities of life and other people's issues.

At the time I was relieved that someone was able to make a connection with me that gave me a ray of hope and direction. Before speaking with her, I felt like my whole world was crashing down on top of me. All of the pain and heartache was coming full circle, and I needed to find a way to deal with it because my way was clearly not working anymore.

I began to consistently work on myself, and even though it was an expensive experience, it was necessary and worth it. The sessions weren't cheap, but I went to over 6 months of weekly therapy and began to work on Sydney Harrison.

I learned through all of the sessions that I have a beautiful heart despite what I have endured, and had a lot to offer the world. This is where I learned about the words "forgiveness" and "patience", especially for yourself, and why it's so important to forgive yourself before you can forgive others.

Forgiveness is one of the hardest things any human being has to learn, but when you do, it gives you the power to love and let go of that which has power over you. Patience with self provides mental tranquility. I learned that sometimes in life you have to slow your thought pattern down and stop being so hard about things, especially yourself. I realized that life can be really strange, and you're always going in or coming out of something, so you should be ready to deal with it.

Patience and forgiveness allowed me the opportunity to learn about my conception, and even though it was still hard, I continued to try and embrace it from the prospective that it wasn't all about me. It was also about my birthmother and I knew that she needed me. She needed to see me strong, and she needed to see that something beautiful could come out of such a horrific event. The beauty of what I learned was that love has the power to transcend any deficit in life. I am so appreciative that my life was saved.

Our mission in life should be pretty simple-how do we improve and save the life of someone who is in need? It can't be done without an act of love. As I began to realize that I wanted to do something really great and have the chance to impact the lives of others. I thought what greater way than to do something in Africa. The children face so many wars, and they are orphaned as they fight to embrace love that can transform their lives forever.

I also believe in the philosophy of the three P"s: Passion, Perseverance, and People. You must have Passion for everything you do in life and belief that it can happen despite what anyone says. You must have the Perseverance to continually work hard at what you believe in. Keep challenging yourself to be the best and overcome obstacles despite how difficult they may seem. Finally, you must have a sincere love for People and understand that we are all human and make mistakes, but we must have forgiveness for today and great hope for tomorrow. It is your love for people that will also allow them to love you. These three components are necessary to reach your dreams.

As I close this chapter in my life, I want to be clear about the significance of my relationship with Monica. Even though I was hurt and not pleased with the outcome of our relationship or the way it was handled, I really respect her and the relationship we had. I'm sure that she does not know this, but she prepared me for the process of truly beginning to address my past and understanding forgiveness.

Sometimes, it is amazing what relationships can do to and for people. I am a firm believer that we have the ability to grow the most when we are at our most vulnerable, as painful as it may be. Relationships tend to bring out our biggest vulnerabilities, even the ones that we may have forgotten about or knew we had.

I have only truly been in love once in my life but Monica taught me to never compromise my self-worth in a relationship, regardless of how strong the love is. In many ways, I admired her, especially her drive and commitment, but she definitely made me deal with things that I truly did not want to address.

From that moment forward I was determined to achieve all that I aspired to. I challenged myself to fully embrace love and to impact the world. In challenging myself, I thought about how to take a negative experience and turn it into a positive one. Monica's abrupt departure left a sour taste in my mouth and I was tired of focusing on that. I felt that it was time to put my energy into different pursuits.

5

South Africa
(Sowing the Seed)

I realized that the time had long passed for me to understand and chart a clear path for where my life was going, what and who I wanted to be, and how I was going to get there. This was especially important because of my son. I knew that fathers were supposed to lead by example.

My son's mother and I never married, but we have tried to maintain a cordial relationship for our son. We had Jerrell at a very young age. We did not really know each other, even though we had dated for over year when he was born, and at that age, we honestly didn't even know ourselves. When you have a child, you have to realize that they did not ask to be here and didn't ask for the parents they got. It doesn't take a genius to have a child, but being a parent, loving and raising a child, is a much bigger task. You do a lot of growing up…quickly.

I love my son more than life itself, and I just hope that he can learn from my pitfalls in life and understand I tried to do the best I could. Even though things did not work out for me and Jerrell's mother, I am so thankful that she brought me the joy of my life, and for that, I am forever grateful.

As adults, most of us have completed the requisite schooling, probably gotten entrenched in a job, started dating, got married, had children…and that's it. I wanted more, but more of what, and would it take to finally make me happy?

I was offered an opportunity to apply for a program that would take me to Soweto, a Township in the Republic of South Africa. Based on what I learned over the years about South Africa, Nelson Mandela, and many other important figures from the region, I knew I would be facing a new type of education and one of dramatic proportions. I couldn't wait.

Prior to leaving, I sat down and spent some time alone with my thoughts. South Africa? What was I looking for? Why was I going? What was the motivation behind making such a trip? After doing my share of personal investigation and soul searching, I came up with the only logical answer I could find- I was seeking Sydney. Myself. Where that would lead, I didn't know.

You may be thinking, why go to South Africa to find yourself when you could likely go somewhere much closer and less expensive to do the same thing? I needed to take this trip, in particular, to help fill in some of the gaps left behind by my cross-racial adoption. Although the racial bigotry I experienced was difficult, I truly believe it strengthened my soul and my perspective in life. Through my cross-racial adoption, I had the opportunity to experience different people, different backgrounds, and different cultural settings in America, to a greater extent than most.

I truly believe that as people, we are more alike than not, but we tend to allow minor differences to divide us. I was not raised that way at all. I was raised to love humanity, and I always wanted to take it a step further and experience other cultures abroad.

Does going to Africa still sound extreme? Maybe, but my life was a contradiction of extremes, and I firmly believed my search for my center would be over upon touching African soil. If everyone had the opportunity to "reach back" so to speak and return to the place of their origin, historically, we would find more of ourselves than we ever thought possible.

You just can't duplicate this experience by reading a book or doing an online family tree search. Understand, I am not knocking those methods, because not everyone has the means to take such a trip, and doing something to discover your past is better than remaining uninformed and unaware. Even still, I firmly believe there is an undefined, inherent value in making a real connection with oneself through the eyes of those who are somehow a part of you. Everything about me is a combination of my parents who brought me to this Earth and I wanted to be as sure as I could of who I was before going any further in life.

I like to research everything first, and with all I have been through, I started to ask myself what had I done to help make a contribution to helping children grow up in loving environments with loving families.

My life was spared and changed forever through adoption, but what about the children all over the world who have been abandoned, orphaned, and have no family to call their own. Then, I began to ask myself if I was ready to challenge myself by confronting my past and helping others in the process.

I wanted to help children in need. I also wanted to raise awareness of the fight against AIDS. I know it was a very lofty goal, but I knew that Africa was facing some very alarming AIDS numbers, and for me to sit back, knowing my story, would truly be a travesty. It would also be an injustice to my family, because they had given so much, and I needed to return the favor by sharing that gift with the world.

Today, there are over 15 million children in Africa that are orphaned due to rape, poverty, disease, war, famine, and abandonment. Children are the essence of who we are and what our future will be. It is up to the adults to set the tone and get involved through helping to educate one another. I felt that there was so much to be done. I worked as a volunteer with an organization called Veronica's Story Foundation, and it was through them that I was able to share the details of my trip. In my first transmission to my parents after arriving in Africa I shared all the pertinent details about my flight and spoke to them at length about what I saw there.

Today, I served in the baby haven where no child is over Four years old and the youngest is only three weeks old. I was surprised to see the boys in the haven that were so happy to see me and immediately began calling me Uncle Sydney. It was pretty clear to me that family is a staple of the community at large.

Some of the stories of these children are heart-wrenching, but its life and the people here are trying to provide a solution to better the quality of life for everyone involved. Mom, you would love this place because they play with and take such good care of the babies, and they drink lots of tea, like you do.

One of the babies was literally thrown away; he is six months old with beautiful eyes. He's HIV negative, healthy and seems to be a good baby. The mom just did not want him. There's another that's two years old. His mother tortured him and he has physical scars all over his body. He has a prosthetic eye, but if you tickle his tummy he smiles so brightly that he lights up a room. Another child is thirteen months old and he is HIV positive. He plays by himself and doesn't interact a lot with the other children but he's a good boy.

One of the other boys found himself in a situation similar to the one I found myself in. His mother just left him in the hospital and never came back for him; however, when he saw me, the first thing he did was wave at me and smile. Though he was very young, about sixteen months old, he seemed to have a really strong sense of who he was and maybe even what his circumstance was, though it's doubtful. I signed the letter, Love Jerry.

I may not have mentioned this earlier, but Jerry has been my nickname since I was a child. It's short for my middle name, Jerome. People called me Jerry growing up, but I really love the name Sydney, because it was my grandfather's name. My mother loved her dad so much, and she shared his legacy with me by naming me after him. Now, his legacy lives on through me. I understand the importance of what the name means to my family, and I am so honored and humbled.

As you can see by my first letter to my parents, my focus was immediately on the children. I didn't mention anything about everything else I had seen, because I had such a focus on them. I knew there were many other beautiful things to witness, but I was on a mission and that mission was to find my true self and be a part of the solution, so to speak. Though I was very tired from the trip there, I knew I was only scratching the surface of what would prove to be a life-altering and rewarding experience.

Not many days passed before I began writing a blog. I wrote the blog for many reasons but one very important reason. I wanted to show the world, especially my friends and family members, that there is so much more love we need to give. Children of the world are suffering while we live in abundance. We live in comfort while there are children out there struggling for just a chance in life.

In the message that was conveyed on the blog was, here's my South Africa experience. I am sharing this to give you a real understanding of not only my experience but what life is still like for the people living in the Township of Soweto.

My First Day in the Township of Soweto

Tuesday, June 30, 2009

My First Week

It has been about a week here now in South Africa and at times I have been floored and moved to tears by what I have seen and experienced. I was quickly awakened to the reality these children face as they struggle for life, for love, and for survival.

I have been changing diapers and rocking babies to sleep. I attended a birthday party for one of the orphaned boys. I will call him Oma, as we need to change the babies' names for their own protection. This birthday party was very special because Oma is one of the babies who tested positive for the HIV virus. He turned one year old on last Friday.

Through our donations we were able to give him a Barney doll that sings. While we can't save his life, a simple toy can offer a sick child a lifetime of joy.

On this same day I met Miracle and at the age of nine she is simply breathtakingly beautiful, but her beauty couldn't even hide the ugly truth that had already chiseled away at her innocence.

Miracle watched her mother die of AIDS, but not before being beaten at home, along with her even younger brother who would often be ordered to the outhouse for hours. There they would stay with little food and no one to look after them. Miracle is now in desperate need of her own miracle as she too has tested positive for HIV. And remember, she is nine years old. But...even in her youth, Miracle has the faith of the ages.

Each night before she goes to sleep she prays that she will be healed of her illness and she prays her little brother will be spared the fate of the virus.

She then begins to sing, "This little light of mine, I'm gonna let it shine..."

Wednesday, July 1, 2009

Soweto Blues (or so it would seem…)

The living conditions…well, I have never seen anything like this before. Families crammed in one-room shacks, living their lives below tin roofs with rocks stacked on them from blowing off during violent storms. Some folks don't even have a roof at all to keep them dry. For those families, a bright blue tarp will do.

As I stepped out of the vehicle and looked around, all I could see were dirt roads and row after row of these shacks…just five feet from each other. And the families who lived there were the lucky ones…because they had shacks!

It's estimated that almost five million people call Soweto home, whether they live in a house, a shack or on the streets. I gathered myself and began to pass out donations. But, as it turned out I wasn't giving them just to children. I ended up handing out donations to moms, dads, children…everyone.

The toddlers were so grateful for the simplest of gifts. Their eyes lit up to receive a pen, pencil, a toy or a T-shirt.

I watched a woman roll up pieces of wet coal to form bricks so she could sell them, hoping to make enough money to feed her family, and all she asked me for was an American pin for her baby. As I placed the pin on her child's tiny, filthy soiled shirt, I said to the mom, "Do you know what this is?" She answered, "Yes, it means peace." The American Flag pin went next to a vintage 1960's peace sign that the child was already wearing.

She thanked me and asked me to take a picture with her which I was happy to do. I fought back the tears as I considered the irony of this unusual yet symbolic moment. Here I was, an American with so much and having overcome my own personal trials as an orphan. I stood there in that village a world away where many are just clinging to life, but they seemed happier.

Friday, July 3, 2009

Game Day Lesson, or Lesson for Life?

Today was game day for the youth soccer team I attached myself to. We got into a van heading for the Soweto Community Soccer game. When we arrived I couldn't help but be taken aback because the field was just plain old dirt.

Well, let me revise that—there was also plenty of broken glass, trash, old hoses and belts from old, discarded vehicles, and yes, two soccer goals. Wow, this is the field we're going to compete on?

There were no lines marking the bounds but there were twenty two excited kids ready to play the game they loved. So we cleared our minds, put our game faces on and played the game.

The Soweto Team was losing in the first half, so Coach Lucky and I explained to the team that they needed to be more aggressive. We told them their positions on the field. With five minutes left in the game we were still losing—but then— with only forty-five seconds remaining they poured it on with a penalty shot and scored! Then a young boy on our team ripped a shot from about 25 yards away to get the go ahead goal and we won the game.

What a feeling!

For all the adversity these young boys struggle with from day to day, something as simple to others called a soccer game was life to them. The chance to compete and the opportunity to be a part of a team, the opportunity to be great for a moment, and the chance to feel alive was worth more than any amount of money.

Tuesday, July 14, 2009

Biking Towards Bliss...

Today while repairing some bicycles at the haven for children, a little girl came up to me and uttered three simple words that had a great impact on me and showed me that I had made an impact on her as well. She said, "Uncle Sydney...I missed you."

I had missed her too as I had been away working with a different group of children but it was clear, a bond had been established and that made me feel great! The feelings I had been experiencing, both good and bad were beyond words.

Moments later, another child who had suffered as many as twenty-seven broken bones because of abuse ran up to me and gave me a big hug, then in a soft and vulnerable voice asked, "Will you be my daddy?" She was only four years old and I was not only speechless but engulfed with unparalleled sorrow.

I didn't have an immediate answer for her and I couldn't help but be moved by her unbroken spirit. Here was a child who had been physically abused and brutally beaten, seemingly by someone who was supposed to love and care for her, yet she still desired a dad of her own to love, and to love her. I was deeply moved.

I asked the House Mother to take a walk with me so I could collect myself and absorb all I was experiencing. It was clear to me I was in a delicate state as so many things and situations swirled around me. As we walked along she talked to me about love and how love never fails no matter how hard life knocks you down; I had experienced that throughout my formative years with my family, and I was seeing it in action through the precious and unspoiled eyes of these children.

She believes, as I do now that with love, this four year old and all of the children here will be okay. I might not be her daddy, but I can be a positive male figure in her life. There are very few male volunteers at orphanages. Here, as in other places, tending to children is seen as women's work; however, I believe if more men would take up the cause of children our society, our world, and our collective consciousness would improve dramatically.

I can relate to many of the children here regarding having a difficult start in life. Thanks to the nurses who cared for me, the doctors who saved my life and the family that adopted, raised and still loves and cares for me, I know that anything is possible. If my heart can be healed, so can hers.

As I walked back to the haven, the little girl was riding her bike, smiling, without a care in the world. She yelled out, "Thank you, Uncle Sydney!"

I smiled on the inside.

Same Day (separate entry)

The other day I did something I haven't really done before; I shared my personal adoption story with some of the children I serve. It was a way to build trust and to my surprise I built some trust of my own.

About one hundred twenty five boys and girls play soccer here at the center in Soweto. I helped teach and coached some of them. Soccer has always been a game that I love and now I had the opportunity to share it with them. But today, before we started playing, I decided to open up my mouth, and my heart.

As I began speaking to the children, I couldn't help but drift away, lost in their wide eyes. They were spellbound and so was I, but for different reasons. The children were all aged three to eighteen years old and although they were overcoming their own challenges, they were so open and eager to share, to learn, and to bond.

I was again taken aback by their forthrightness, strength, and inner-beauty. My heart was full. Although we were born in some cases decades apart, at that moment, a bridge had been forged and connected us in a way that would last a lifetime.

If for one moment I wanted to feel sorry for myself about how I came into the world and had to suffer, their sobering realities put everything in crystal clear perspective and clarity very quickly.

Tuesday, July 28, 2009

Who's the Role Model Now?

I have achieved a number of firsts on this trip. The one I am most proud of is being the very first male volunteer to work directly with the children. I am thankful to have had the opportunity and I know it has had a positive effect on the children and an even more positive effect on me.

If you think about it, the greater significance is these children have rarely had positive dealings with men. Often, the men whom they have encountered physically hurt them in some way.

I have been called a trailblazer here and have come to really embrace the title and the role. These children need to see, to know and to believe that men can be loving, and patient, and kind, and decent without exploiting them. The young boys here need to see and to know what being a positive man is all about.

My dad always told me that a man's word is all he has, so do what you say. He taught me that you'll be judged by your actions in life. I was lucky to have a man, a good man guide me down the right path and set my feet on the path of knowledge...and a strong hand to keep them there. It was still difficult at times for me. I can only imagine what life is like for these boys here.

It's my job to take what I have learned and use it to gently push these boys and girls to be their very best in spite of their circumstances. It has become my job for however long to show them that they can achieve everything they desire through hard work, perseverance and faith.

I explained that they needed to remove the word, 'can't' from their vocabulary and replace it with "can".

It's amazing what growth can happen when you challenge yourself to deal with things, and go outside of your comfort zone. That is what happened to me. In spite of, or maybe because of, my life circumstances, the children of South Africa caused such a change in me. I am a part of them. Their story is my story.

There were many times before when I believe I was given signs, but chose not to acknowledge them or ignored them when God was trying to speak to me, and to my heart. I doubt that I was still enough to know when God was seeking my attention. I thought about my time in Africa, and I reflected on a time in my life in my professional career when God was speaking directly to me on a personal level. It was at a time when I was in the prime of my plumbing career. It took place shortly after the tragedy of 9/11. During the drive I thought about the families and people who had been affected by 9/11 and how life is not promised. I was still mulling it over as I pulled up to the home and got out and knocked on the door.

The homeowner answered and responded with a very polite hello. She told me that she was having an issue with her toilet downstairs. She went on to share that the toilet had been working improperly for the past couple of days. She mentioned that her daughter and daughter's boyfriend rented out the basement and that they would take care of the payment and could answer any questions I had, because she had to get to work. I let her know that I would take care of the problem and would let her know what the outcome was. I had no idea that I was getting ready to come face to face with a situation that was going to open my eyes and heart about the importance of time and life.

I walked downstairs to check out the problem and saw that the toilet was overflowing each time you flushed. But what was different about this time from thousands of other toilet stoppages I experienced was the water inside the toilet bowl was a faint pink. It was like someone had dropped food coloring down the toilet, or that is what I wished it was. The water began to rise and I shut off the toilet valve so no more water would fill inside the tank. I began to say to myself something is very wrong here, it just did not feel right.

I removed the toilet from the floor and took it outside to take it apart. I'm not sure what made me take it outside to disassemble it, but it was the first time in my plumbing career when I've sensed danger. While I'm outside trying to get the bottom of the situation, the boyfriend is nervously pacing back and forth asking me what's wrong every five minutes. The homeowner's daughter also followed me outside to ask if I found the reason for the stoppage. My spirit told me to tell them that I needed to get a part, then get in my truck, drive around the corner and then break the toilet. I did just that.

As I drove, my heart began to beat faster and faster. I parked the truck, got out and then began to take the toilet apart. I cracked the porcelain and then saw the most disturbing thing I've ever seen. You might remember that earlier in this chapter I shared with you that there is no way I could consider my story so unique when there are so many with stories similar to mine. What I found that day taught me a valuable lesson about life. The blockage in the toilet was what looked like a fully-developed baby to me.

The homeowner's daughter had flushed her new born baby down the toilet. My heart sank as I called my boss to tell him about what I had found on my first plumbing call of the day. My boss was very concerned about me because he knew my story. He instructed me to lock myself inside my van and said he would be there in a few minutes. He called the police and told me to not go back to the residence; he would take care of everything.

My thoughts immediately went to this young baby. I wondered why the child wasn't wanted and why the young woman made the decision she made. Each of us has the responsibility to make a difference in someone else's life. I consider that to be a great blessing, but some people just don't seem to understand how precious that is. I learned later from my boss that the young woman who aborted her baby on her own was charged with murder.

The new born baby was at about its eighth month of gestation, and already had oxygen in his lungs. I took some time off from work to clear my head and gather my thoughts following the incident. I now know that God was speaking to me through that. He let me experience it so that I could see that I was blessed and how I must share my blessings with others. God knew how special I was and just what I was supposed to do with my life. I consider that moment to be the one where I fully understood that I have a calling. This memory was especially vivid during my time in Africa because I spent a great deal of time thinking about humanity, life and serving others.

I took very vivid photos from my experiences in Soweto. I look at them from time to time and shake my head in disbelief. It has been nearly two decades since Nelson Mandela was elected president of the country and slightly longer that the practice of apartheid had been ended. Even though it appeared that this would have promoted great change, seeing the conditions of the Soweto Township, and the continuing despair on the faces of the people made me wonder when real change would come.

I do understand that things will not dramatically change overnight and possibly not even in my lifetime, but there's always hope. It seemed that in spite of the regime, and the attitude change by many, someone's finger was on the pause button and the march toward equality had stopped dead in its tracks.

My thoughts often turn to a woman who explained how she and her young children scavenged for wood scraps to build their one room shack. The shack had a doorway and a rooftop, and she was very proud of it. I looked inside the doorway of her little shack and saw it was actually made of the façade of an old Pepsi sign. It's amazing what people can do with so little.

Education is a gift in South Africa, and the children there are in school for what seems like the entire year. They do not have a Board of Education, per se, nor do they have a large bureaucracy overseeing matters of teaching and learning. What they do have, however, are massive communities of people spread out over miles and miles, all living in squalor. It is almost impossible to fathom. This, in addition to other issues, makes a cohesive educational system very difficult to sustain.

As the days drew to a close and, the temperature dipped to cooler levels, I would often stand outside and watch the sunset, wondering how things were back home and how everyone was doing. I contacted my folks frequently, because I missed them. I missed home, but I was there to do a job and to see what change I could create for the people there, as well as, myself.

On my final day, I made sure to visit with each of the children and the staff and made sure to embrace each and every one of them. I wanted to remember their smiles, the sound of their voices, the smell of their skin, and the reflection of hope that gleamed in their eyes.

I felt both a sense of relief and dread as I came to the realization that I would be leaving them behind. I am sure they have seen many people come and go, but for me it had become personal. In spite of the obvious losses they had suffered in life, they still opened themselves up to embrace me as a family member.

As my time in South Africa came to a close, I wasn't sure what the complete takeaway would be for me. After all, I had been there for just over sixty days, and forty-seven of them were spent on my hands and knees crying. I wasn't crying just because of the fact that the children were suffering, I was also crying for myself. I had been so selfish in thinking that my situation was unique, and there I was among a considerable number of children who had been beaten, raped, abandoned, stricken with the HIV virus, and even dying from AIDS.

It was a sobering reality that gave me pause as I reflected on my life and what I had intended to do with it going forward. My Christian belief tells me that God is everywhere and knows the suffering of His people. I believe that, and I don't question it, but I do question the lack of action being taken to protect children and other vulnerable people.

Broadly speaking, what does my trip and my experience in South Africa say about us as Americans? It's difficult to fully say, because the two countries are so vastly different, but in some ways South Africa can serve as a mirror for reflection on our actions in my opinion.

America shouted shame at South Africa for apartheid, yet we too have a great deal of blame and responsibility in addressing our own issues concerning race, gender equality, and racism. The South African people have so little, yet they will sacrifice everything for an education. Education is a gift and a blessing in this country and is too often taken for granted.

South Africa fought for the right to have democratic elections and even today, has record turnouts for voting. Many fought in this country for the right to vote, yet we often still struggle to get people out to vote.

The quest for happiness through family, despite the squalor and despair, is apparent in South Africa. On the other hand, the goal for many in America seems to be the attainment of happiness through material gain.

I'm not at all suggesting that we're any worse or better than South Africa or its people. For all of the seemingly negative attributes of America, I can't think of another country where most people would prefer to live given the opportunity. The bottom line is that each country has its own problems, and I'm not sure there's enough time in the day to debate how each country can either individually or collectively solve its problems.

If there is one problem I believe we as people can really solve it is the issue of poverty and hunger. Based on what I was able to see for the few months I was in South Africa, there are more than enough resources to go around, but again, the have-nots are many, while the haves are few.

Sound familiar?

In the end, as I took stock of my life in its totality, my biggest question was, *if I died today, what would my legacy be?* Would I have been simply known as a person with promise, gone too soon, or something more? Did I try to help someone, or was I so busy wallowing in my own self-pity that I couldn't see anything or anyone else?

I needed people to know that I genuinely cared about others. I had to build that theme around my present and future. South Africa was necessary for me to continue on this quest.

6

Returning Home

I sat in the Johannesburg airport dazed and confused, watching the planes taxi onto the runway. As I waited, somewhat impatiently for my flight, I thought about all I had experienced and wondered how I was going to feel once I actually took off, heading back West. I sat with my hands clenched around my ticket and stared into space.

It wasn't a moment of celebration, neither was it a moment of sadness or sorrow. I'm not really sure what to make of it, but my mind and body seemed to somehow separate, metaphorically speaking. The best way I can explain it is surreal. All of the confusion I endured over the years was starting to become clearer. All of the negative experiences that ultimately turned into blessings gave me pause to consider my life in its totality and offered me a perspective I never had before.

It is typically different for men than for women, but every person goes through a metamorphosis of sorts. I could feel this metamorphosis happening as I was heading toward becoming a part of the establishment, that group of adults we, especially as young people, didn't trust and didn't want to become. There I was, over thirty and finding some balance, but I still wasn't sure that the path I was taking would ultimately make me happy.

Gone were the paralyzing feelings of abandonment and not knowing how to open up. The past sixty plus days on the ground in South Africa had changed me even more than I could immediately appreciate. I will leave it to others to tell you whether or not the change was for the better, but I certainly feel it was.

I watched the news on the monitors above my head in the terminal and saw CNN and the BBC News on different channels. I don't even remember the stories being covered, but I do remember the logos and my feeling of excitement at seeing cable TV for the first time in a few months. I smiled broadly and even chuckled a bit as I thought about how significant, yet insignificant, the importance of cable TV was to me in that moment.

A part of me was just looking for something familiar, something that would give me a sense of normalcy, so I could re-acclimate myself to life at home in America. One thing I was sure of was that a part of me had been changed forever and would never be re-acclimated to my sense of normalcy.

It would not be enough for me to return home and fall back into the same life I had prior to leaving. I was changed and had decided I was going to do something with my life that would make my family proud. Even more than that, I wanted to touch the lives of my neighbors and friends alike.

My flight was called, and I looked around as a number of people stood up in the enormous waiting area. I had become so consumed with my solitude that I perceived it to be approximately a twelve by twelve space with only a few people when in fact, there were closer to several hundred people preparing to board a massive 747 jet sitting next to the jet way.

As I was waiting for my turn to board the flight, my emotions were on overload. I reflected on the personal victory I had achieved and it became overwhelming. I was leaving a country that no one in my family had ever visited and would not likely visit. This isn't because they didn't want to but because carving the opportunity out of your life to do it can be very difficult. I made history, in a sense, and basked in that light for just a moment so that I could give God all his due.

As I boarded the plane and took my seat, I looked around at the immense size of the aircraft cabin and marveled at the technology that allowed this behemoth of an airplane to take off, let alone stay in the air. I was watching a TV show called <u>Myth</u>

Busters and watched as the engines of a parked 747 blew over a Lincoln Town Car. The sheer power of the engines alone made me a believer and any fear I had went right out the window.

I could hear the pilot or a crew member let us know we were about to take off, so I buckled myself in and braced for takeoff and a very long flight. As the plane taxied down the runway, picking up more and more speed, I heard the growl of the cavernous engines. The massive plane began to lift off the ground and leap into the air, immediately banking, as we flew toward the sun.

Sitting on such a large plane for a long period gives you time to think, and think I did. I thought about the faces of the kids and parents at the orphanage, as well as, the happy memories I would keep for a lifetime. As the aircraft continued on its long journey I noticed that we were crossing the terminator from day to night, and I finally settled in to sleep. I was having trouble relaxing and asked a flight attendant for a cup of tea, which she brought very quickly. I needed it.

What I found most interesting and pleasing about the experience was how accommodating everyone was to me even though I was seated in coach. As I thought about it though, I realized it made sense. Who would want to be bothered with a bunch of uncomfortable passengers on a nineteen hour flight traveling half way around the world? On a flight this long, I am sure it's much better for the crew when the passengers are comfortable.

There was an interesting buzz in my ears as we flew along. At first, I thought it was just my ears popping from altitude changes, but it was actually the hum of the 747 engines that seemed to settle in for the long flight. They were neither revving hard nor were they scaling back, it was just steady. Along with that buzz was a pulsating that was so steady you could write a symphony to it. Eventually, the calm, steady sounds caused me to drift off into a deep sleep.

I was surprised to awaken and find that we had returned to the U.S., and my thoughts turned to seeing my parents and everything I wanted to tell them the moment I got off the plane. I thought about it for a minute and wondered whether I was really prepared to debrief or whether I should just take some time to absorb it all before speaking about it in any great length.

The best thing about traveling abroad is coming home. Interestingly enough, I missed home so much it wouldn't have mattered where I was. All I wanted was to grab a burger and a beer--the type of food I liked and missed so much while I was away. As I walked through the airport I looked at the many advertisements and photographs around me.

I had been through airports a few dozen times for various reasons, but this time was different. I was reacting to the culture shock I had experienced. As much as I would like to tell you I was fine, I wasn't. It wasn't because I was sick but because I was different. Not so different that I was losing my mind, but different in that I had lost "something" and I wasn't sure if I wanted to get it back. Oftentimes, when we lose something we've carried all our lives, even if it is for our good, we suffer a type of withdrawal that makes us want it back simply because it's familiar.

I went into the men's room to get myself together, and as I washed my hands and put water on my face, I looked in the mirror and didn't recognize the person looking back. Clearly, I had not gone through any major physical changes during my trip. My weight was fairly steady and I wasn't injured, but the Sydney Harrison that left for South Africa was definitely not the one that returned.

To say I was different seems generic and maybe overly dramatic, but it was true and it was the only way that I could describe it at the time. I needed to know exactly what had changed, so I began to give it serious thought.

My family met me at the airport, and after exchanging handshakes and hugs, I got in the car and started home. The feelings I had about them before I left seemed to have intensified upon my return. I was in love with my family.

I especially appreciated how much I loved them after seeing how precious life was in South Africa and experiencing the true value of life through the eyes of the children. I wanted to be absolutely sure my family knew how much I loved and appreciated them. That became very important to me.

Obviously, my family didn't *have* to adopt and embrace me the way they did for so many years, but we were way past that and the fact is they were indeed my family no matter what circumstances brought us together.

My attempt to somewhat debrief myself before speaking with my family proved to be more challenging than I originally thought. Where would I begin? Life had taken on a new meaning for me on so many levels that I found it almost impossible to fully discuss South Africa, Soweto, the orphanage, the children, and their many stories in a way that would really express what it was like. I was overwhelmed and felt like a dam about to burst.

I attempted to write down my thoughts and feelings but so many of them were conflicted, and it became more of a chore than a labor of love. Though I think my efforts to chronicle my experiences were valiant, I found myself falling short of what I wanted to convey. A lot of that had more to do with my own inability to fully understand what I had experienced more than it did my actual ability to write it all down.

Back home at last, and I immediately walked into my home and recognized all of the familiar trappings I had left behind several weeks prior. Everything was as I had left it, including some clothing I had neglected to put away as I was rushing out to catch my flight to South Africa. While I was back in familiar territory with every modern convenience I was used to, I thought back to the children of Soweto again.

Hopefully, by now, you're noticing a recurring theme-the children. I had been so affected by my experience that I was having difficulty getting it together once I arrived home, even though it was a place that was very familiar to me.

My family came in with me. Normally they would have stayed around to talk to me more about the trip, but they must have seen something because, almost in an instant, they told me to call them after I had gotten some rest and left. I know what they saw, and it wasn't just exhaustion from the trip. They were witnessing a transformation in progress, and I'm thankful to them for being able to recognize it, because I didn't.

I felt like I had been changed, but I still wasn't fully sure how. I began to consider how I could serve my community, churches, schools, friends, and just about anyone that may need my help in some way. Yes, I had been changed for the better, but for me, I was just walking in my purpose now that I had found it.

I thought I was going crazy. I lie down on my bed, put my head on the pillow and began to remember the living conditions I had just left a day or so before.

Suddenly, my "things" weren't so precious or important anymore, and though I was not about to have a mass give-a-way, I knew that I would take a different stance on how I viewed material things going forward.

I thought about my former girlfriend. She was so consumed with material things that she thought it best to simply walk away from me during the period when it was difficult for me to provide them. I am not saying that there weren't other factors, but this was definitely a big part of it.

While I was away, I decided that I could not take what she said and how she said it as a negative, personal attack. I had to evaluate the situation and my response, and use it to make myself a better person. I now recognize that the person I ultimately became would have made us incompatible anyway.

Sometimes we put so much emphasis on our homes, cars, and other things that we lose sight of what's really important. I knew for sure that life was about far more than material gain, and I was going to live that philosophy. Don't get me wrong, I don't think money and material things are bad, I just refuse to allow them to cloud my thoughts, friendships, and integrity.

In my room there were dozens of magazines and other periodicals I had kept. I looked at them and could see the faces of Americans that looked similar to the ones I had recently seen in South Africa. The only difference is that the Americans were standing outside of homes that had been foreclosed on or were close to it.

I knew sleep wasn't going to be an easy thing to accomplish, so I got up and took a drive around the neighborhood to try to relax and collect my thoughts. Though I had only been gone a few months, I started noticing more and more houses for sale, rent, or padlocked by the sheriff due to foreclosure. Something had changed even during the short time I was away. I was not happy about it, and it definitely did not seem to be for the better.

The auto industry collapse in Detroit directly affected the entire country in some ways, but it seemed so far away. This time, it hit much closer to home. Prince George's County was in a serious crisis, and I was wondering more and more what could be done to help the people who were in need. I didn't quite know where to start, so I simply started by talking to people.

I have always been a social person and never had trouble meeting people. Some would say I have never met a stranger, and that's true. My parents taught me to embrace people and not to turn a blind eye or deaf ear to people in need. I was already predisposed to being that way because of everything I experienced.

On the other hand, I also know that there have been many with situations similar to mine that have gone the other way. Some have decided that since they were dealt a raw deal in life or since no one ever took care of them, they are going to take care of themselves and not care at all about others. I did not want to be that guy.

As I spoke with resident after resident, it became crystal clear that many promises had been made and broken. These promises came from local, state, and national politicians who frankly didn't have a clue about solving a problem that had been decades in the making.

Bad mortgages and greedy banks were big reasons for the collapse of the housing market and, much to our detriment; a great number of people in Prince George's County got into bad mortgages and lost their homes. I wanted to put a stop to it, but I didn't know how.

I didn't have the money to financially bail out every person and frankly, not even one person, but I knew there was *something* I could do to serve the public trust. I began to go throughout the community to see what I could do to lend a hand to those in need. My actions would catch the attention of a man who would eventually become my mentor, political father, and friend.

As a native Prince Georgian, I attended school in my community, and had lived my entire life there and had started a business there. Prince George's County is my miracle, my pearl, my home, and my promise. When I say my promise, it is not just some slogan or cliché to me. It is the true promise that was instilled in me to do some great things on this Earth however I could and be of help to as many people as I could.

I was given a second chance at life when all seemed lost. I felt that I owed a debt that I could never repay in a lifetime. I made it my business, mission, and vocation to come as close as I could by being the best person, son, and friend possible.

I remember having a conversation with my mentor, where I shared my desire and passion for loving and helping people. I was willing to be held accountable for that, and he told me I sounded like a true public servant leader. I told him I was interested in running for office, more specifically the position his boss was vacating. To say making such a statement was bold and even ballsy is an understatement.

At that moment I committed myself to running for public office. As I stated earlier, politicians go into politics with the best of intentions but in a lot of cases manage to lose their way. This is generally because of an overzealous need for money, power, or some combination of both. I was determined I wasn't going to be one of those people.

My mentor went on to explain that I needed to surround myself with positive, smart people who were equally committed to me as a candidate and as a person. He also told me something that horrified me and for some reason I hadn't thought about before--I had to raise my own money and the competition I was facing was fierce. While I was not a stranger to helping people, this was different. I would be pressing the flesh with the masses and taking it a step further by asking them to trust me, a relative unknown. It was a daunting task indeed.

My mentor's name is Dr. David J. Billings, Chief Deputy Clerk of the Circuit Court of Prince George's County, MD. At the time of our chat, he was the Chief of Staff for the Council Member of District 9, which was the position I decided to run for. The position was vacant due to term limits.

One thing I hadn't exactly counted on was the reaction of my family, particularly my Mom. Dr. Billings came over as I was making the announcement to the family, and while everyone was generally supportive, my Mom was skeptical. She mentioned I had been through so much disappointment in my life, and she could not stand to see me hurt if I did not win or dragged through the rigors of a contentious, nasty, political fight.

There was an open and honest discussion about how I would be packaged and rolled out to potential voters. For a while it seemed surreal, because discussions were going on around me as if I was not even there. I am not certain if I was generally nervous about running or specifically concerned, because like many other things and situations in my life it was uncharted territory. Ultimately, for me, it just became another challenge to overcome.

7

The Campaign

(Accountability)

My election bid for office got its start in my mind well before I left Africa. I didn't officially decide to run until I returned home and learned that it was a real possibility. The fact that I truly wanted to run, and could maybe even be successful, propelled me into action. It was eleven months away from Election Day, which was scheduled for September 14, 2010. I immediately began forming my committees which included a treasurer, campaign manager, campaign consultant, campaign policy advisor, and campaign field manager. You may be thinking, *why so many people?*

Simply put, it's impossible for one person to manage everything in a campaign. This includes keeping track of donations, managing finances, scheduling events, returning telephone calls, and conducting research, among other things.

Look at candidates you've seen over the years, and you will notice that those who have been successful have had adequate staffing and organization to make sure their candidate didn't stub his or her toe while walking through the minefields of a tough campaign. On the other hand, those who have not been successful and have run into trouble didn't. They may have had an idea, but they lacked the resources and organization to make it a reality.

I was poised to pull off one of the biggest political upsets, not only in Prince George's County, but quite possibly in the state.

You see, my opponents were well known, but I was unheard of, so any noise I was able to make was a major accomplishment that was not only good for my campaign team, but for the county. It offered people an opportunity to meet a virtual unknown with great ideas. They had a real and distinct choice coming from a voice they had not heard before. Though I was known around the county because I had lived there my entire life, I knew garnering endorsements would be next to impossible to achieve.

I knew that no one wanted to donate money to someone they didn't know and who was untested, but I also knew that I was a genuine people person. Excuse the cliché, but I really do love people. Being a people person has its advantages especially in my professional field of real estate.

I believe one of my greatest assets is my ability to communicate true understanding to people, so running for this office made perfect sense. I truly believe the people needed a candidate that focused on the constituents, and who really heard and cared about them.

Friends and family routinely reminded me of my strengths and shared in my vision of addressing poverty, growing small businesses, creating jobs for people in multiple sectors of the community.

I was excited and scared at the same time, because even though a political career can affect change and be very rewarding, it can also be a cut-throat business. It was very important that I protect my family as much as I could. I understood the issues and concerns of the community, and I believed they were not being addressed in a way that could move the county forward.

It seemed as though anytime I spoke to someone I was in campaign mode and began to give vignettes of speeches that would ultimately become campaign slogans, advertisements and 60-second promos for my candidacy. I was ready to give everything I had for the ideals that I believed could create positive change.

My days began at 4:30 am in the morning by listening to inspirational and motivational talks on CD, as I showered and prepared myself for a series of incredibly long days. After I dressed and put on my campaign attire, consisting of a suit and tie, I made my way to the various local metro stations.

Like New York and other major metropolitan areas, our Metro system is the method thousands of people use to get around the area from Northern Virginia and Washington, DC to the surrounding Maryland counties. I would go to different metro stops to meet with constituents. Meeting them there with bottled water, a handshake, and a smile often went a very long way in getting them to know who I was and in building my political brand.

I was surprised at how welcoming and open many of the people were. I was further surprised at how willing they were to offer their opinions about issues within their individual communities and how effective, or not, my opponents were over the years in addressing these issues.

It was valuable information that no amount of money could buy. When I heard two or three dozen people expressing the same concerns within the same area, it caused me to especially take note and appreciate the urgency of their concerns.

One of the biggest things I learned while campaigning is that if you really pay attention, you will learn just about every life lesson you'll ever need to know. You learn about honesty, integrity and jealousy, and you quickly find out who your friends and enemies are.

You also experience the joy and pain that comes with giving and serving. Although there is indeed joy in serving, there is also the pitfall of realizing there are so many competing interests you'll never be able to please everyone. That being understood, it becomes exceptionally difficult to manage the minefield of trying to make decisions based on need rather than political gain or personal favoritism.

Little did I know that soccer, the sport I loved, would be so helpful in preparing me for my run for office. As a soccer player you are constantly focusing on a ball that's being kicked around a very large field, and it seems like everyone on the field is always running at full speed. When I think about it, all other sports have scheduled "time outs" that coincide with the game itself or television, but soccer doesn't. Once you start running, you don't stop until the ninety minutes is up.

Also, as the ball is being kicked and shifted from player to player, you have to have to anticipate where the ball is going before it gets there in order to make a play for it. You have to trust your teammates and coach to work together toward a common goal.

I wonder what the statistics are for those who have played a sport at some point in their life and the connection to politics. I don't doubt they would show that people who play or have played sports, in many cases turn out to be more successful, ambitious and focused than those who did not. It seems like a very logical connection.

One of the most important lessons I learned from playing sports is how to lose with grace and how to deal with adversity. I have played in games where the other team jumped off to a big lead, and we had to play our way back. Win or lose it always showed the team what kind of character we had as players and people.

In politics there are some people who really do care much more about power, influence, and agenda, than focusing on the primary task of serving others. In soccer, as in politics, you must stay focused on being a help and benefit to others for the achievement of a positive common goal.

Never stopping until it's over, keeping track of everything around you, working together for a common good, and pressing on when things seem hopeless are all traits that the sport of soccer and politics share. Although I had never run for office before, I felt somewhat prepared.

When I was growing up, my father and I had conversations about life all the time. I remember having such a conversation with him after I had just been suspended from school. He wanted to connect with me in a way that he knew I could comprehend. He said, "son, if you took five of your most successful friends in school and tried to be like them, you will be a product of your environment, and begin to excel in school and in life."

As the campaign kicked into full swing, I found out very quickly that politics is a very fluid thing. There's a lot to be said about situations happening very quickly, in real time. Things were moving forward at such a fevered pace that it had gotten to the point where I would often forget to eat. My days were lengthening, so much so that I would often forget the time or even what day it was. My days would generally border on a twenty-four hour work day with very little sleep. I was constantly on the go.

Meetings had become the norm, and it seemed as though I always had a meeting with someone, somewhere. Aside from members of my campaign team, I often met with and repeatedly thanked volunteers who gave a great deal of their time for no pay. I counted it as a blessing that they were so willing to give of themselves and believed in the ideals and platform I ran on.

I also knew I was probably on my way to digging a deep financial hole, as I was using my own money I had saved from my various business ventures. Taking out a loan was not an option. Going into debt for the sake of winning the seat was not a palatable idea. It had gotten to the point where I had to form yet another committee that was instrumental in raising money for my campaign. I hated having to be so focused on money, but it was necessary to continue my campaign and get my message out there.

Seeing that I was always so busy and ate and slept the campaign, Dr. Billings, my mentor, would have me over to his home and made sure that I ate, rested and had an opportunity to decompress. He kept me grounded and would often speak with me about the downside to campaigning, especially the media and how perilous it was.

I began to understand the media for what it was. For many years, candidates have used media to sway and shape public opinion. This was certainly true with my candidacy. They could paint a picture any way they chose and while I was a newcomer and someone with a great deal of tenacity, the media wasn't particularly kind regarding my candidacy. A friend of mine talked to me about one of his college professors who taught journalism. This professor was a bit rough around the edges and said that if someone is talking about you, good or bad, it is a good thing because you are either the topic of conversation, or were at least in the conversation. His point was that when they stop talking about you is when you should worry.

Dr. Billings often fed me with a long handled spoon, primarily because he didn't want to overwhelm me. He had a lot of wisdom and knowledge to offer but providing it all before I was ready to take it in would not be fruitful. He knew this which is why he always felt it was best to give me advice as needed, a little at a time. He must have sensed something was coming, because my foray into the media spotlight, though on a local level, consisted of attacks.

I would be leaving out a big part of my growth if I did not take the time to fully express how pivotal and important Dr. Billings was in it. I have had mentors, teachers, tutors, and work colleagues, but Dr. Billings was different, he understood me. I remember him speaking to me when we first met, He said:

> "Sydney I just wanted to tell you about the fabulous event you had. It was such a fantastic evening. I am so appreciative that you invited me to the affair. I thought your heart was in the right place as you spoke to the crowd about the importance of the situation with orphans in Africa and how you raised money for those orphans. I just want you to know from this point on we are friends."

Here is a man that was seasoned, has paid his dues in life, and still wanted to share his wisdom and knowledge with me and be my mentor.

At the time, my father was one of the only people that would take the time to teach me lessons of life. Now, Dr. Billings had become one of those people, and he began to share his life lessons with me, as I shared my goals, ambitions, trials and tribulations with him.

I needed a new set of eyes to help guide me through the path of life, and Dr. Billings showed up. He is such a major part of who I am today, because he taught me the true importance of reaching back and helping others on your way up the ladder. I remember him making me promise that everything he teaches me about life, I would pass on to someone else. He said, "share these lessons I teach you Sydney, because you did not get there on your own." He was right.

At that time, the Prince George's County public school system was ranked among the bottom in the state. Our county had grown quite significantly over the years, while certain issues continued to grow along with it. I began to think about ways to address how poorly we have done on standardized tests. I also spoke to parents about the reasons they took their students out of Prince George' County schools and found ways to place them elsewhere. It was very eye-opening.

I also saw how our population was ballooning, but our public safety and infrastructure were not growing along with it. I began to really understand the issues surrounding foreclosures in the county, and it was clear that we were only at the cusp of the housing market's downward spiral. I saw the need for small businesses in the county to create a border tax, and I also saw how desperately we needed jobs and opportunities for locals. I did my best to address these issues.

My life had become campaigning, so much so that I began to sleep, eat, and breathe the issues and possible solutions that could move the county forward. I surrounded myself with people that completely understood these issues and educated myself very well on each one of them. I devised a slogan for my campaign that we believed had a catchy ring to it---"Vote The Same, Get The Same."

The reason I believed in that slogan so much was because, whenever we vote candidates into office year after year, their campaign promises remain the same but then, so do the conditions they promised to change. The obligation and responsibility of an elected official is to be a servant of the people. An elected official must put their ego to the side and serve the people.

My belief is that once you lose or ignore your ability to learn, your ideas and ways become outdated and stagnant. We must always maintain our ability and desire to learn and never become so arrogant to think that we have all the answers because we never do.

A candidate must show the ability and willingness to listen, reason, compromise, and be transparent. This shows continuous growth and the voters appreciate it. The job of elected officials is to improve standards and quality of life for constituents through thoughtful legislation, not propelled by the officials own agenda and greed, but by a love for people.

Being flexible is the key to being successful in just about everything we do in life. I learned the importance of that growing up with my family. You have to be able to adjust to new situations, ideas, and circumstances if you really want to be successful and achieve your goals. You can't let changes or diversions impede you.

I began to study local, state, national, and international affairs. I attempted to build partnerships with other candidates and elected officials but I quickly ran into multiple road blocks, because no one seemed to want to play with the new kid on the block, especially not early in a campaign. At the time, it was just me and a very few volunteers, but no one believed I was going to make any serious noise or shake things up.

Many nights I would wander into the office to try and get some last minute things done and often found myself waking up there the next morning. It wasn't a case of me trying to prove anything to anyone. Frankly, no one really knew about it, because I never talked about that part of campaigning. It just wasn't that important considering my ultimate goal.

One night, while lying down listening to the night animals run around outside, I asked God to give me the wisdom and knowledge that I needed to run the race. To me, simply asking God for a win is akin to having unrealistic expectations. I know that God is not a genie and certainly doesn't exist for my selfish desires, so I just prayed His will be done in my life and for that of the county.

A typical day after sleeping in the office was no different from any other day. I'd already have clothing there, and I was able to shower and shave. I'd dress and zip out of the office, often headed to Dunkin Donuts to grab some donut holes for constituents. I would also have bottled water, all of my campaign materials, buttons, pens, and anything I could carry.

My campaign workers would often meet me at different metro station stops and my campaign chairperson would make sure I always had some food delivered to me. She was often worried, because she noticed I was losing a considerable amount of weight. The funny thing was that being hungry didn't bother me, mainly because I was even hungrier to keep running a successful campaign. Unfortunately, that's another one of the pitfalls.

The real estate market began to dip south everywhere, and from time to time I'd call on my friends and former colleagues to see how they were doing. In spite of their personal and professional difficulties, they all managed, in their own way, to let me know they were proud of me and of the job I was doing. I had to make people believe, and it was beginning to happen. The talk on the street became the Sydney Harrison campaign, and nothing could have made me happier. People were talking and that was exactly what I needed.

My team was running like a well-oiled machine as we raised funds and quietly placed ourselves in position to become a front-runner. In a campaign where there are ten candidates you had better find a way to be noticed. My website suddenly gained traction as well, with dozens of people signing up to be volunteers. Then, suddenly, paranoia kicked in.

Almost out of nowhere, I started noticing that I was paying particular attention to everything around me. I wasn't worried about someone attempting to hurt me, but I was concerned about spies from the other campaigns that might try to sabotage me. It was a surreal feeling but definitely not an unreasonable one. I knew that in the arena of politics, anything was possible.

Things had gotten so crazy that I began to limit the amount of information being disseminated as well as the number of people who had key information. This is not something I wanted to do, but life experience had already taught me not to trust so I found myself in familiar territory.

I read something once about Nelson Mandela before he became President of South Africa. As one of the senior prisoners on Robben Island, he began to foresee and practice how he would govern if he were elected. No one could have anticipated that he would spend nearly 30 years in jail only to be released, become president, and then forgive those who had all but enslaved an entire country for decades.

I was terrified of the open forums that were held around the county. It was an opportunity for the public to meet candidates, ask questions, and learn more about them.

The issue I had with these forums was that you had absolutely no idea if the people in front of you were actual residents, plants from other districts, or even from plants from some of the other candidates themselves. The danger in this situation is the question and answer period of the forum. During that time the questions are not given to you in advance and nothing is scripted, so it would be very easy for another candidate to pass along a question for someone to ask that they knew would be disparaging or just impossible to answer.

One of the funny things about these forums is that the candidate has only two minutes to give a complete answer when given a question. If you've watched any debate on TV you know there's no hard and fast rule to that, because sometimes it's just not possible. I tried to stay within the time parameters but there were some questions that required significantly more time to answer. Other questions just were not appropriate for that type of forum, because they required something closer to committee hearings for consideration before being answered.

One question I was happy to be asked was about political entitlement. Basically the question was about why some people felt they should be elected, especially if they were already in office and things had not improved. When answering the question, I made sure I stood firmly and spoke clearly and concisely so nothing I said could be misconstrued.

My answer centered on leadership and being prepared to represent the county. It also discussed that the right candidate should have the ability to inspire people. It's up to the common citizen to use their judgment and decide who they can and will trust, or not. The will of the people must not be polluted, perverted, or twisted to suit the candidate and their agenda. If a candidate is able to focus on the issues at hand and stay focused after being elected, I don't doubt that we would see our country move in a more positive direction with thoughtful legislation.

Once I had completed my answer, the crowd began to clap, slowly at first and then to a thunderous applause. People were standing and cheering, almost as if they were at a sporting event. I had solidified my place as a respectable candidate to be reckoned with and to be taken seriously.

One of the things I actually began to enjoy about the forums was spending time with the other candidates. I began to learn their body mechanics, posture, general responses to questions, and desire to listen to the responses of other candidates. It really gave me an understanding of the types of competitors I was dealing with. In real estate sales as well as plumbing, you had to know your client, think quickly on your feet, and problem solve. This experience came in handy.

Hearing the other candidates' questions and responses allowed me to make adjustments to my message so that it would be delivered with more clarity. It reminds me of the adjustments made going into a second half of a game. As I began to warm up to the process, I tried to make sure I drove the important points home, spoke about the things I was informed about, and highlighted the benefit of my strengths and the danger of the other candidates' flaws.

I truly spoke passionately and from the heart. We were all asked questions about the issues our county faced, ranging from education, public safety, jobs, foreclosure, and housing issues to healthcare, and our beloved veterans. The challenging part was to answer the questions with substance when you only have two minutes to answer.

I remember being asked a question on education and thinking, I need at least fifteen minutes to answer this question. I was the only candidate that had attended and been a part of the Prince George's County public school system. I personally experienced the flaws, overcrowding, and closure of good schools due to poor funding. Speaking about this issue was my passion, and I learned to deliver this powerful message in two minutes.

I had arrived at the point in my campaign where, if one of my fellow candidates wanted to hurt me they'd have to spend a significant amount of money to do it. I was reaching people by word of mouth, and it was proving much more powerful than any TV commercial spot or radio advertisement. Political contests are to be taken seriously, and you can't take it personally. You must remember that it's a competition that should be dedicated to service, not winning and personal gratification.

I knew I had to be convinced and convicted of my politics and purpose, because I had a bull's eye on my back. I was not connected to any political team or machine like many of the others, so I was pretty much on my own.

President Obama ran his campaign on the ideal of change and I was excited as I watched his climb to the highest office in the land. As for his message of change, some people believe it's something that happens overnight instead of something that happens over time with persistent and constant effort. People should decide what they want out of a candidate, but more importantly, and much more significantly, what they want out of their lives. Change is something that must happen within each of us before it can be spread throughout our communities.

My candidacy was being endorsed and my mind became focused on a new set of goals. I had to begin looking toward behaving more like an elected official and not just a candidate. While there was a significant amount of time left in the campaign, I needed to re-focus myself and let my constituents know that I was electable.

I was returning phone calls, thanking people for endorsements, kissing babies, shaking hands, and speaking just about anywhere people would have me. When cold calling constituents I found myself falling victim to some of the issues that have plagued candidates for centuries. While there were some who embraced the call and pledged support, others would be angry and say some pretty ugly things.

There was a serious lack of trust in politicians, especially within our county. Much to my misfortune, my candidacy was coming on the heels of yet another county scandal that made everyone cringe. I won't go into specifics about it, but it was so egregious that it made national news. This even further heightened the citizens' distrust of public officials.

I had more than four hundred signs strategically placed throughout the county, spots on YouTube, and a presence on the web through my campaign website. Things were moving right along, but I was entrenched in everything that was happening and was actually looking forward to the end. I had some time before the campaign would be ending, but the days were moving faster and Election Day was coming that much closer.

As Election Day approached, every candidate believed they had the race wrapped up. There were lots of confrontations between candidates, but I managed to stay above the fray. One main issue for me was my health. I now understand why so many candidates either drop out of races or end up in the hospital after it's over. I had lost twenty eight pounds and wasn't eating or sleeping well.

I missed my family, because I was always gone somewhere and interestingly enough, I was right in my own community-just not at home. My young son was a huge consideration because, he was a teenager and I knew he needed me. I hoped he understood what I was doing and why I was doing it. Though I had explained it to him, it is a lot to ask a family to expend so much emotion, energy, and time on the hopes and dreams of one.

After another long, all night work session which ended with me again sleeping on the office floor, I began thinking of the strength and intestinal fortitude of a young, pregnant, teenage girl, homeless and eating out of trash cans. All I could think was, *God is good.*

Unbeknownst to my birthmother, she set this moment in motion by making the decision not to have an abortion, in spite of the many difficulties that went along with carrying a baby. The name, Sydney Harrison, was printed on placards, pens, T-shirts, posters, refrigerator magnets, and just about anything you could print on. It was surreal, and it came with a heavy price. There were many days and nights of heartache, but there were also many days of happiness. The pain and despair of a child became hope in the man I had become.

I was and will forever be grateful. I promised God that His plan for me would be realized before my days ended on this Earth. I know He didn't allow me to get as far as I have only to fail.

As I got off the floor of the office in the waning days of the campaign, I thought of all the sacrifices that had been made by so many on my behalf. Then, I knew for sure that every campaign dollar and every penny of my own money spent could not begin to repay the love of community, family and friends.

The next day was Election Day and I realized that I really had given it my all. Regardless of the results, I worked just as hard as all the other candidates, I formed new relationships, and above all, I learned so much more about life, family, community, and love. Every day, I prayed myself to sleep, submitting my love letter to God. I would ask that He guide my footsteps in life, and I would thank Him for His unyielding love. I thanked Him for His mercy and for giving me this opportunity to serve.

I might have lost the election, but my heart was open. I knew that this was my opportunity to really serve my community in some capacity, and I was determined to never give up, never stop dreaming, and never give up hope. My faith rested on this determination and above all, GOD.

I realized I was here to make a permanent impression on my community and its members. It was my calling to represent them and fight for them, even if I was not elected. It was my time to give back and sow seeds in my community.

Life is always a new chapter and understanding that, you should always work to grow and evolve. Always remember, it's not where you start in life, it's where you end up. It's about the impact you make, for the good.

Sometimes in life, you have to figure out how to make a rose grow on concrete. Life will sometime give you hardened soil and ground, but it's up to you to not let this harden your heart.

Going forward, I am anxious to get back on the campaign trail and try again. What will be different this time? Everything and nothing. I say "everything" because I've already made an election bid and learned a great many lessons from the loss. I say "nothing" because my focus, beliefs and reasons for running have not and will not change.

Throughout this story, I have given you a front row seat to my life, the people that I love, and the people that love me. As I bring my life narrative, thus far, to an end, you will see how the people I have told you such much about, have matured and evolved into the beautiful people they are today. I want to share with you their success and determination, as well as, where I am in my life at this present time. The bottom line is that we are all still pushing, still dreaming, and most importantly, still loving. We did not let the past dictate our future but allowed it to mold us for what life has in store.

My parents are still business owners in Prince Georges County. Their company, Pioneer Realty, is still going strong. They are both past presidents of the Maryland Association of Realtors and were the first husband and wife to ever be nominated as president. My brothers and sisters are all married and raising their children. They also continue our parents' vision by being pillars in the community.

My birthmother Jody has weathered the storms of life and has seen her way to brighter days. She is now drug-free, has a successful marriage, and has adopted a child. She has received a second chance at life and has continued to give back to communities in her local town by serving the needy, helping the homeless, working at the women's shelters, and serving in her church.

As for me, I am currently a realtor, helping people build upon their dreams through homeownership. I continue to serve on several foundations and organizations within my community, galvanizing the most important component in a community—the family.

Since my own campaign, I have volunteered on several other political campaigns. I currently serve on several community based non-profit organizations. I am most proud of my affiliation with Saving Our Children, which primary mission is to work with adolescents to develop coping, interpersonal, and life skills. I am also a board member of W.H.A.L.E.R.S Creation, an organization that works tirelessly to promote foster care and adoption through the arts and media.

I still firmly believe that our youth are the future, and we must, as a community, make this our priority. The campaign has ended but my dedication to serving the community has not. In many ways my life has come full circle and I know that everything in my life happened just as it should to make me the person I have become.

Afterword

As I think about my life and everything I have been through, I came to the realization that I am the embodiment of what love is supposed to be. I think about the unconditional that we are supposed to exemplify to one another. Have we lost the concept of family and community, or have we just forgotten?

The most important foundation of humanity is the family. With the love of family, hard work, and determination, dreams become realities. Two more important things we need in this life to succeed are patience and forgiveness. Above all, we cannot forget the act of service. The act of service is to reach back and pull someone along with you as you climb your ladder of success.

As a society we idolize the electronic age so much that we have forgotten how to relate to one another. We see how our nation has suffered as a result of the banking, auto and housing industry collapses, and at the same time, we continue to tell our children to go to school, get a good education, get a job, find a career, get married, start a family and become a productive member of society. Unfortunately, this message is falling on deaf ears as we have let go of the ideals that have made this country great. We have to get back to them.

I remember a conversation I was having with my parents as I began this arduous journey. I knew they were getting weary of my search for my birthmother as well as my desire to write this book. I asked them to please trust me and this process. It was not solely about finding my birthmother or about this book. Rather, it was about love, and humanity. Life is a precious opportunity, and we are charged with the responsibility to never stop dreaming and never stop believing. Above all, we must never fail to realize the beauty within each of us.

When we understand our purpose in life and allow our belief and passion to drive us toward our goals, our zeal and desire will provide us with the fuel we need to fulfill our individual and collective dreams. It takes time and a great deal of effort to achieve greatness, and not one person can achieve it alone, but when we work together as one, greatness can shine on us, and the world.

Sydney Jerome Harrison

Special Thanks to Jocelyn Smith; Memories 2 Be Photography for providing cover image.

If interested in learning more about Sydney and what he is doing in the community please feel free to visit
www.Soulsearcherbook.com

Made in the USA
Middletown, DE
19 February 2021

34010057R00076